Divining Dante

Divining Dante
Recent Work Press
Canberra, Australia

ISBN: 9780645009057 (paperback)

 A catalogue record for this
work is available from the
National Library of Australia

Cover image: 'Dante Alighieri' Image from page 656 of *The poetic and dramatic works of Alfred Lord Tennyson* (1899)
Cover design: Recent Work Press
Set by Recent Work Press

recentworkpress.com

Divining Dante

edited by
Paul Munden
Nessa O'Mahony

Contributing editors:
Priya Sarukkai Chabria
Moira Egan
D.W. Fenza
Paul Hetherington
Alvin Pang

RECENT
WORK
PRESS

CONTENTS

UNITED KINGDOM

IRELAND

INDIA

Foreword

Dante Then and Now

It was a life that had—and still has—political, popular and poetic dimensions.

Most of Dante's works—including the *Divine Comedy*—were the product of his banishment from his native city. He was, as he mentions in the *Comedy*, born and baptised in Florence; this was some time between late May and early June 1265. It was there in the early 1290s that he composed his collection of poems and commentaries, portraying the development of his relationship with Beatrice: the *Vita nova*. Later in that decade he embarked upon a political career and was elected to high office in the city at the turn of the century. In the *Comedy* he dates his 'middle of life' crisis to 1300, since around then he fell foul of the Papacy and Florentine political rivals and was subsequently sentenced to exile (1302). The rest of his life would be spent under the protection and patronage of various rulers of other cities and regions in Northern Italy; and while this would involve constantly 'going up and down other men's stairs', it would also lead him to compose works such as a treatise on vernacular poetry, an unfinished philosophical encyclopedia (the *Convivio*), and the *Comedy*, which he began around 1307-10. In one of those Northern Italian cities, Ravenna, he died, 700 years ago, in September 1321.

Dante's writing during those years of exile constantly reflected his political commitments. Not only did he write forceful invective in the *Inferno* against political opponents in Florence and corrupt Popes at Rome and Avignon, to make them, as his ancestor in Paradise would say, 'scratch where they itch'; he also developed a positive vision of renewal in the governance of Church and State. Early in the second decade of the fourteenth century, it seemed that there was a faint chance of uniting much of Europe under a new Holy Roman Emperor, and Dante responded to that moment in public letters and in the political utterances of the *Purgatorio* itself. That project ended in failure, but his concern for political and religious reform continued to be voiced in his final works. Around 1317 he wrote a treatise on world monarchy in which he also argued for the restriction of the Church's temporal power, and even in the *Paradiso*—the journey of celestial enlightenment that concludes the *Comedy*—there is a constant regard for the earthly order; for time as well as eternity; for the human as well the heavenly 'populace'.

The wider earthly populace has always been part of Dante's readership and audience. Although he speaks of his challenging voyage through Paradise being followed by only 'few', nearly all of his verse is in the Florentine vernacular, not Latin; and an epitaph written very shortly after his death describes him as 'the author most loved by the people'. From Dante's time to the present the *Comedy* has been appreciated by a wide range of readers, and it has been publicised by performers, from Boccaccio lecturing on the *Inferno* in a church in fourteenth-century Florence, to Benigni reciting in twenty-first-century town squares and theatres.

Writers and artists of all sorts have continued to respond strongly and frequently to Dante's work, and the *Comedy* has produced a vigorous afterlife in the popular genres of the novel, drama and cinema. The *Inferno* especially still generates compelling visual imagery in the form of illustration, film, video and graphic fiction. Translation of the *Comedy* into languages from Arabic to Yiddish testifies to what has been called the 'generosity' of Dante's text; and some of the translators have themselves been poets. The versatility of Dante's vision and language—and his power as a precedent for ambitious projects—has been appreciated by poets from Chaucer to Heaney and beyond. Dante himself entered into dialogue with other poets in the early *Vita nova* and in the afterworld encounters of the *Comedy*; and the voices in this collection make clear that the dialogue still goes on. As one of the poets in *Divining Dante* observes, *amor mi mosse, che mi fa parlare*—Beatrice's words at the beginning of the *Comedy*'s journey—still start us off after seven hundred years.

Nick Havely

Introduction

This latest volume in the series of themed anthologies from Recent Work Press marks the 700th anniversary of the death of the acclaimed Italian poet, Dante Alighieri, whose life and work Nick Havely summarises so expertly in his Foreword. As with previous anthologies, we decided to take a numerical approach, with 70 poets chosen to write their responses to Dante's masterpiece, *The Divine Comedy*, as it has become known. Seven poet-editors contributed to this process, gathering work by poets in their geographical regions. The result is a remarkably diverse assembly of poems by both established and newer voices from around the world.

In a year when we also celebrated the 200th anniversary of John Keats, for whom legacy was a notion 'writ on water', it is poignant to consider the extraordinary legacy of Dante. The idea to create this book was born when the world was just beginning to be convulsed by pandemic, and many looked towards Italy as the European country mostly badly affected by the first wave. Dantean imagery of purgatory and inferno weren't hard to find in those early news reports from the regions worst affected, and we all gradually learned to assimilate those notions into our own experiences of pandemic. But this wasn't intended to be a book of responses to the Covid crisis, nor was it an act of translation. *Divining Dante* is intended to show how Dante's influence has shaped the sensibilities of writers around the globe.

Numbers are fundamental to the *Comedy*, in every aspect of its structure and thematic detail, so it seemed appropriate to adopt numerical thinking in our approach. We even set a 70-word line limit. We envisaged structuring the anthology to mirror Dante's three books: *Inferno*, *Purgatorio* and *Paradiso*, but we also had a hunch, and a concern, that poets might focus disproportionately on Hell. Our solution was to invite each poet to submit three poems, one for each of Dante's books. We would select a single poem from each poet in such a way as to balance the anthology. All three poems from each contributor would be available to read online.

Our intentions, however, were put to the test by the wilful ingenuity of our poets.

When taking stock of the submissions, it quickly became apparent that our structural scheme would not work. For one thing, quite a few poets submitted a single poem in three parts; splitting such a poem would clearly be problematic, and if it fell within the 70-line limit, we gave it full admission—an act of gatekeeping logical yet quirky, and perhaps controversial. The major change to the original plan was to group poets by country. A pragmatic decision, it has—we hope—enabled the poetic styles and preoccupations of each country to be appreciated more distinctly. Within each section, the Dantean order remains the guiding principle, with the triptychs and more idiosyncratic contributions blended in.

There are no direct translations of Dante here; that work continues to happen plentifully elsewhere. But many elements of Dante's work are nevertheless *carried across* in these poems. As Nick Havely suggests, Dante's ideas, language and sheer poetic ambition continue to inspire. Some poems take quotations from the *Comedy* as their starting point; others weave famous images and phrases into their new fabric, some explicit, some highly 'slant'. For those familiar with the *Comedy*, these references will be clear; but even for newcomers, certain things may well resonate, such is the extent to which Dante's imaginative vision has entered the popular 'language' of many artforms. For Italian readers, particular phrases from the *Comedy* are as well known as lines from Shakespeare are for the British, an astonishing fact, given that a closer historical comparison would be with Chaucer; Dante's advanced model for the general Italian language remains quite extraordinary.

Within the anglophone world, it is Dante's images and concepts that reverberate today more than the figures of speech. It may seem strange that such a religious poem should connect so strongly with our relatively secular age, though it's useful, perhaps, to consider the associations of the latin *religio*, eg *religare*: to bind; we are bound, after all, in a multitude of ways. But whatever the doctrines or beliefs with which we choose to bind ourselves, many of us retain at the very least a metaphorical allegiance to the concepts of hell, purgatory and paradise. Our use of the term 'hell' or 'hellish' may sometimes be banal (and our reference to 'paradise' often commercial), but we—humankind—are strangely proficient at creating various, veritable hells on earth. Some are depicted within the poems here: Auschwitz, with a sign over its gates like Dante's Inferno; the wartime fate of Hiroshima; the events of 9/11—a date that will never need a year in its stamp. In a quieter vein, the trauma of dementia is also featured. Prue Shaw, in her book, *Reading Dante: From Here to Eternity* (2015) identifies the connection precisely:

> [Cavalcante and Farinata] know events that are a long way off,
> but as these events get closer or actually happen, this knowledge is
> extinguished. This is one of the most cruel and refined aspects of the
> punishment of the damned, punishing them as it does not in their
> bodies but in their minds. Their state seems like the experience of
> dementia. (28-29)

Purgatory, too, is a term we tend to use with somewhat flippant association, but certain current scenarios—particularly that of quarantine, and the ongoing plight of refugees—are highly pertinent, and feature in poems.

It is Beatrice, the love of Dante's life, who takes him to heaven, and love is a theme equally important to those of exile, atonement, and the extraordinary proliferation of human considerations that characterise the *Comedy*. Dominating all of them is a reflection on behaviour, the consequence of our actions, something that is central to almost all poetry and storytelling, irrespective of any religious framework. Dante puts himself centre stage in the reflective process, effectively establishing an intricate entanglement of biography and poetry, an experiment that continues to this day.

Another aspect of what Dante achieves that has increasingly defined what we expect of poetry is the physical geography of the poem. Dante's philosophical musings and imaginative flights are rendered within poetry of extraordinary vividness, grounded in imagery that is startlingly naturalistic. 'Show don't tell' goes the classic creative writing mantra; it might have been invented by Dante himself. The most bizarre, 'unimaginable' scenes are presented as if with cutting-edge CGI.

There's huge respect, but also a degree of irreverence, in this anthology. 'You've failed with me. I'm still a heretic', writes one poet. 'You had some really crazy ideas, Dante', writes another. And if honest, many of us would agree. But crazy ideas are of course what we now rely on poets to deliver, taking us into unchartered territory, 'amalgamating disparate experience', to use TS Eliot's phrase (1932:287). The work in this anthology is a kaleidoscope of disparate backgrounds, experience, and other influences. In the mix are the Lindy Hop, the Birdman of Alcatraz and the Paradise Movie Theatre. Maybe that's unsurprising. Who, though, would have predicted two separate servings of Chardonnay?

As with the 2020 anthology, *No News*, some poems here reflect on the Covid pandemic, featuring the various accoutrements of lockdown, face masks, sanitised hands, tiers, and of course a critique of politicians—with Joe Biden and Kamala Harris offering an uplifting glimpse of better times. Contemplation of time itself is fundamental to Dante, who, by setting his poem in 1300, manages to look both forward and back. The engagement of 21st-century poets with that process is a natural extension of Dante's own thinking.

Some of the poems here use *terza rima*, the rhyming structure that Dante invented. Clive James (2013) has commented that it is impossible to sustain a long poem using *terza rima* in English, arguing that it clamours too much with its own virtuosity (or not), never achieving the seemingly effortless quality of Italian, where rhymes are so much easier. That's probably true of the book-length poem, but some pieces here make use of *terza rima* to remarkably good effect. There are other formal offerings, notably sonnets, as well as looser forms—and prose poetry, the popularity of which is surely at an all-time high.

So-called 'free-verse' (of which prose poetry is perhaps the most extreme example, being free not only of a formal rhyme scheme but also all aspects of poetic lineation) is essentially the freedom for a poem to take on the individual form most suited to its purpose. In creating a poetic form so utterly original, Dante may be seen to pave the way for every idiosyncratic poetic offering. He devised something of the highest formal sophistication; equally, he *conformed* to nothing. And prose poems, increasingly, do not conform to any one idea of what a prose poem should be. They even carry secretive rhyme. Clive James refers to Philip Larkin's belief 'that good poetry doesn't rhyme just at the end of the lines, it rhymes all along the line' (xii), and perhaps where 'lines' don't even exist.

*

All the poems included are in English of one variety or another. We have used our publisher's spellings as default, but poems from American authors retain their difference. We gathered poems primarily from English speaking parts of the world, but we also considered it crucial to have Italy involved. Special mention must go to Moira Egan, who not only brought Italian poets to the project but also translated their work herself. And rather than follow the alphabetical order of countries, we begin with Italy and follow the sun.

We should like to thank all our contributing editors—Moira Egan (Italy), David Fenza (US), Paul Hetherington (Australia), Alvin Pang (Singapore) and Priya Sarukkai Chabria (India)—and of course all the poets who embraced this project so wholeheartedly and with such distinction. We hope you enjoy reading the work presented here, and the larger compendium of all the work submitted, which Recent Work Press has made available online.

It's unlikely that any of the poets included in this anthology hold any kind of believe in their divine purpose. In a secular sense, poets continue to pursue exceptional paths of their own, but their principle aim here is rather to celebrate the remarkable influence of Dante Alighieri, and beckon in other writers and readers who may well think Dante too 'difficult'. 'As usual, I was going to skip Paradise' is how one of the poems here is titled, though other poets have remarked that it's *Purgatorio* that people like to 'miss out'. Part of our purpose in compiling this anthology is to draw new attention to Dante's *Comedy*, and encourage people to read the whole work, to skip their habitual skipping. It's a poem that defined the colossal scope of what poetry might do, and it's surely folly to think it's not for us. As Basil Bunting wrote, 'On the Fly-leaf of Pound's Cantos' (1978:110): 'There are the Alps ... you will have to go a long way round / if you want to avoid them.'

Paul Munden and Nessa O'Mahony

Works Cited

Bunting, B (1978) *Collected Poems*, Oxford: Oxford University Press
Eliot, TS (1932) *Selected Essays*. London: Faber and Faber
James, C (2013) *Dante, The Divine Comedy,* London: Picador
Shaw, P (2015) *Reading Dante: From Here to Eternity*, New York: Liveright Publishing Corporation

ITALY

So Tell Me…

I. How Did It All Begin?

> *Ma dimmi: al tempo d'i dolci sospiri,*
> *a che e come concedette amore*
> *che conosceste i dubbiosi disiri?*
>   *—Inferno V.118–120*

The book was old and we, perhaps, too young.
Its story had been written (and somehow
this seemed important) in a foreign tongue.

It's true, by the way: you may feel awful now,
but if you summon happy memories back
you'll feel worse still. But since you long to know:

One day we met to talk about the book,
which both of us had read. We were alone.
Discussing the kissing scene was all it took—

our will, by then, was something not our own,
climbing and changing us, as roses refashion
arbors, or notes blank staves, tone by sweet tone.

As for the book, that author of our passion,
we closed it then to make a free translation.

II. What Are You Waiting For?

…ma dimmi: perché assiso
quiritto se'? attendi tu iscorta,
o pur lo modo usato t'ha' ripriso?
—*Purgatorio IV.124–6*

Why bother, now, continuing to climb?
Let others climb, who have the energy.
I'll sit right here until I've served my time.

Between lost youth and far senility
stretches the cage-like silence of these ages.
If only I'd brought my fiddle for company.

Instead I recall old music, passages
scored in my brain … I close my eyes and sway,
hearing each string, feeling their varied gauges,

becoming them—till I am no longer player
but fiddle, instrument being tuned, shriven
of discord, readied for some bow to lay

its body down on mine. Ah, maybe even
I, then, will be translated into heaven.

III. Is Heaven Even Enough?

Ma dimmi: voi che siete qui felici,
disiderate voi più alto loco
per più vedere e per più farvi amici?
  —*Paradiso III.64–6*

My will, these days, is soothed by the caress
of Love's voice, which allows me to desire
exactly what I have—no more, no less—

for if the place I craved were any higher,
then my desire would fail to harmonise
with that high voice whose will has sung me here.

You'll hear, from me, no discontented sighs.
I long to sing my part in Love's chorale,
for Love has willed I won't live otherwise,

and Love's song brings, when I can hear at all,
this peace. Its lyrics are an ancient language,
arcane in meaning (in the original

one noun means *love as charity as longing*)—
but no one translates; you learn it in the singing.

Geoffrey Brock

5

Landscape

...che fece me a me uscir di mente
—Purgatorio VIII.15

I walked over to a branch laden with snow
where the weight of one of the ravens bent the wood
I became that sway of black and gray
and that different green (a mix of frost and sage)
that advanced with a touch of choler through the clouds.

Everything was landscape within that purgatory:
anger: a cairn,
uncertainty: a heap, a hill,
the lack of love: trees with numb shadows.

—Observe—said the shadow in the nearest bush,
—the fog swallows your pain.
Learn in your mortal space
through learning you barely graze heaven—

Yes, I answered, and the light diminished the morning anger
cleaving each body from its resentment
forcing the shadows to be silent, and a sharp light,
blue—was it already paradise?—
took the place of the landscape, of the first person.

Antonella Anedda

three messed–up sonnets

paradiso

eyes of light that cause a storm
yet docile in the idea, troublesome,
of the high meeting of the minds in contact
a white airplane in deep space

eyes of light that lacerate the skies
reawakened dreams of a vanished age
the two of us, raindrops rising
up and up, in a vortex of ellipses

desire focused in the warp of clouds
a lesser god of the weft of bodies
shame in the manifest brilliance

desire focused, the loss of words
finds strength in the void of senses
the subtle voice that rhymes with love

purgatorio

everything burns, love burns
the expectation that haunts everything
thus, inside a cloud of flowers
painful thoughts full of arrows

everything burns, we two at the foot
of a mountain of vanished dreams
waiting for the veins to open
to the new contact, again and again

it is the mind becoming a prison
this closed beach that collapses
you feel the gash, feel the end

it is the mind becoming a prison
the escape of noose-tied thoughts
that makes it impossible to rise

inferno

the bottom is gloomy and all that remains
is the atrocious crash in the bare forest
of fire, mud, and frozen shit
deformed bodies: no one who wins

the bottom is gloomy, the views are sated
with our pain, with our surrender
the two of us distant with no way out
twins buried in naked sighs

down deep down and further down
our eternal condemnation abysses
the absence of sharp light turns to colossus

down deep down and further down
the breath that gave contact is gone
the sound of love whirls, destroyed

Rossano Astremo

Trittico scientifico

At the time of the dolce vita

Unlike mosses and lichens
Cryoconite—that dark sediment
Visible in summer on the surface of the glaciers—
Preserves radioactivity for a long time.
From the glaciers of the Caucasus to the Arctic archipelago,
Passing through what remains of the glaciers of the Alps,
Cryoconite preserves, in abnormal quantities,
Cesium-137 dating back to Chernobyl—1986—
And even the isotopes of plutonium and americium
And bismuth-207 traceable to nuclear tests
Carried out at high atmosphere at the time of the Dolce Vita.
Like the lungs of ex-smokers,
That also remember what their owner has forgotten,
Cryoconite emerges as the beast-conscience of the short century.

The acne eruptions of Eleanor of Aquitaine

Who was the last to leaf through them
For what they were? Larkin would ask
At the news that the prayer books
Have become the breviaries
Of fingerprints.
Virus pestilences tragedies and famines
Open up on a biological horizon
From medieval illuminated manuscripts.
The parchments written on buckskin and deerskin
Are excellent for studying the genetics of animal strains.
They tell a story of migration and human DNA,
Climate changes and viral infections.
Handled, embraced, kissed by thousands of people
Centuries after their creation

Medieval books are a hard disk of monks and scribes,
Noblewomen, poets, and knights
With the nasal staphylococci aurei
And the propionibacteria from the acne eruptions
Of Abelard and Eleanor of Aquitaine.

Erbium and Dysprosium

Erbium and Dysprosium,
The atoms subjected to the great frost,
Have recently entered the Periodic
Table of the Elements:
We got to minus 273.15 degrees,
Very close to absolute zero,
The Italian Research Council proudly asserts.
The properties of the zero friction liquid
Are reached only through the workings of the cold,
MIT echoes, harshly.
And I listen to them with admiration,
My windpipe, too, is curious.
Erbium and Dysprosium are two boys
With very strong magnetism.
They cough a little, then go away.
They return as Cosma and Damiano and they are saints.

Franco Buffoni

Mystical Visions of Saints and Sinners

{ a fragrance trilogy }

Inferno

A night walk in a dark wood. Heartwood hard and hearkened. The crackle and smoke of a fire, just beyond the next hill. Bawls and caterwauls of distant beasts: leopard, lion, wolf. The rank skank of sex and ego, pheromones and fear. You want what you want. Slo-mo slog through slough through sloth. A sudden brush of breeze clicks through the black leaves. A wickedly strabismal glint of topaz. You have never felt so lost in all your life. So you take the hand offered: where you will go is even deeper, darker. The sulfurous scent of descent.

top notes: smoke. rafflesia. fleurs du mal.
middle notes: asphodel. oud. camphor.
base notes: hyraceum. tar. phenol.

Purgatorio

The slippery slope, the *limen*, light or dark. Which pulls you more? The sunset shadows dance, seductive. Red, white, black. Pride, prick and prickle, price or praise. What did you covet, what then did you crave? Just pull away, the way you know you should. O guilt of pleasure, pleasure guilt, the gate. The sweaty climb, sublime, the primerose hill. Presume. Preclude. Prie-dieu. Your epic dreams (wrong epic), gates of ivory and of horn. You postulant, you penitent, you fragile flagellant, you black-strap whip. The deep rose speaks so sweetly yet too well you know its thorns.

top notes: damascena. pomegranate. vetiver.
middle notes: indole. leather. frankincense.
base notes: opoponax. sandalwood. myrrh.

Paradiso

The liquid air is soft and clean; you sip it more than breathe. As if enveloped in white velvet, calm, she takes your hand in hers and guides you on. Her eyes are cobalt, piercing as the noonday sky. You have the sudden sense of being seen: no vales, no veils, no lies. The Sunday bells begin to chime, the Ave's rhyme. The lilting, lulling music: all is perfectly in time. A rose explosion, sunlit notes of innocence and clarity. The light so bridal white it's almost blue; the sweet so sweet it's almost bitter, distant as the stars.

top notes: white rose. aldehydes. jasmine.
middle notes: Chamaelirium luteum. acqua santa. virgin's bower.
base notes: white amber. castoreum. white pine.

Moira Egan

Purgatory

'We have let our sins rot
for the salvation of repentance
and this place is a flatland.

The glory of pride, the sanctity
of lust, honest gluttony
that looks after the flavour ...
and tempestuous anger, a penny
of destruction ... now
equalised with regret,
we are scattered with sloth
which remains, like a city stopped
in its steps by a summer afternoon.

We repented. We did not understand
our mistakes in choosing
the sacrilege of moderation.
Terrible: the tort of those who learn,
the righteousness of those who abjure
with a plumb-line life.

You saw how we are healed
and untouched, faded inks,
healthy and illegible to ourselves ...
Now, the war is over
and we'd turned traitor, just a minute before.'

Paolo Febbraro

E ombra vedi

ma el li disse: «Frate,
non far, ché tu se' ombra e ombra vedi».
—Purgaturio XXI.131-132

Silhouettes, shadows.
And these days, thin shadows,
signals in the brain,
electrical disturbances, at best
pixel icons on screens;
even if you touch them, you don't pierce them.
Bodies and distances, embraces
typed and not felt, hands
that don't recall the squeeze of handshake:
that you are shadow, we repeat
before pressing the red button,
and you see shadow.
And when we're solid again,
will we know how to recognise each other?
Will we still be real?

Massimo Gezzi

in/out

he enters, it's dark, he runs, he follows the rag, he sees it poorly, can't catch up with it, he sees it clearly, wasps sting him, he sees nothing, flies, the wind batters him, crushes him, he falls into the mud, it hails, a dog tears him apart, he comes back whole, he pushes certain stones, he burns in an oven, he comes back whole, he falls into a river, it's made of blood almost of lava, he drowns and they stab him, he becomes a twig, the twig is split, it's torn, he comes back whole, it rains fire, he burns his feet too, he runs again, they whip him, he falls into shit, he beats himself, a stone is punctured, he dives into the hole head-first, they set his feet on fire, they pull him out, they twist his head around, he walks backwards, he falls into pitch which bubbles, pull pull, head emerged, he breathes, they tear it off with hooks, they close him in a bell, he doesn't move, he runs naked among the snakes, they tie his hands, they roast him, they cut him in two, he heals again, they mutilate him, he heals again, he gets sick, he gets covered with boils, he ends up with his head stuck down in the ice, they pull him out, they stick him back in but this time with his head up, they pull him out, they reinsert him, supine however, horizontal, he cries up toward on-high, the tears close his eyes, they pull him out, put him back at random in blocks, cold, a jaw crushes him, he gets swallowed then shat upwards, exit

Marco Giovenale

Lüs da domandà

Send her here to help me,
Lucy herself. She knew
that I couldn't trust
eyes that knew what was wrong
and did not fix it.
I should have put them on a plate,
just like I saw at an altar.
From then on, how you see is changed.
She knows something else, she
who is able to give
whatever is holy in her,
a light that I did not understand
and I kept going, with my wound
that did not heal.
A light to ask for.

She took me by the hand
that I offered her one day
and I awaken
and it is already full day.

I'm on the first step
already spick and span
and under a thin layer
which must be kept polished
I see my reflection,
which confounds me
because I am just like that;
none of my flaws
is hidden from me.
To repent in order to start over.

And I go to the second step,
cracked from side to side.
Here it's my turn to speak,
to say to the angel of God
who has appeared before me
what he already knows.
On the third step, up there,
seven Ps that mark
my forehead.
Seven, to speak of all the sins
that we must purge here.
Seven wounds that can
still be healed here …
To hope. To continue to go
forth. I'm at his door;
in his hands he has the keys
to open the tomorrow
that calls us to look on high.

Franca Grisoni

Dante Fragments

1

Dante has it both ways:
fainting in the book he's writing
at the afflictions he wrote, feigning
pity, not outrage.
The face he wears is shining and suffering.
It's the opposite in here:
we keep our cool as they take our temperatures
with a thermal imaging device
and inside us are strange
languages, venal chatter, high-pitched
pain and fury, the beating
of hands,
the bright, revolving doors of feeling
beyond arrest.

2

Too easy to call it a dream you woke from
barking, and child-you being interrogated:
'Could you do it again would you do it

the same?' and reaching for the tree,
emitting some sort of cry to the leaves
like a needy teething neoman

who prays and prays, while he to whom
you pray sharpens your desire, not
hiding but holding up the thing you want.

Will Schutt

18

UNITED KINGDOM

The Lucifer Event

The crash. The rupture. And the numbness after.
A shudder through time. The planet's history
is trauma: landmasses buckle, fracture and drift. Or

there's a stray jag of space-rock—a momentary
rip in the air, the earth itself a flinching
body. Long ash winter, and things freeze.

No fancy, then, to figure it as violation—
Lucifer's plunge, stabbed deep, like shrapnel
lodged close to the heart. The ocean

flash-boiling away. An unfathomable
void a whole hemisphere shrinks from. Then
the wounded magma gushes up to fill

the great unsaying: an island more fire than
rock at first, then steaming basalt. Mute
buttresses. Meanwhile a splinter-thin

wrongness, rusty skewer through the meat
of us, remains, an abscess, scar tissue
sealing it in like what a child might

still not find words for, groping through
a forty-year night. All you feel is a chill
from the chasm, like touching vertigo.

Don't look down. There is circle on circle
down there, souls' endless repetition
of themselves, worlds turning on a spindle

not of iron, not flame, but cold—a frozen
lake, a wind that locks the ice tears
to our eyes, words to our lips. Negation

itself, all hunger, and the null of gravity.
Almost absurd, the monstrous figure at the core
wedged upside down, now that we come to see.

Philip Gross

Purification

for my father

He lives now in a place
where language belongs to others,
like this autumn garden
with its vines and fountains.
Knuckled blooms, sap drained from the gland.
Late buds like stopped mouths.

Underbrush of brittling stems
soon to be cut down, yet still
giving forth a green that is composite.
Bruised blues, medicinal pinks,
sickroom yellows, dirty-sheet whites, all meet
in the late green of this giving forth.

Leaf fingers splayed and crabbed
make gestures to be guessed at:
sun touches them and they curl
as hands once curled with pleasure—
still would, still do in dreams.
Though speech is lost

he still knows sound. Behind a screen
a bird translates the pouring of water,
stops to draw from the source, and pours again.
Another makes the jab-jab-jab
of clumsy fingers at a typewriter
rousing a memory—he's stricken—

like that day on the dementia ward
when a voice cried *Help me help me*
and he sprang from his chair,
pyjamas gaping, and raised his bony fists.
How the nurses loved him! Jab-jab-jab.
He sighs, and turns his face to the sun.

Winter will purify, but frost
has not yet broken the spirit.
Small bees still chance it
for a taste of late sweetness.

Jean Sprackland

Statius: Purgatorio XXI

I grow mountains from moles on the back of my hand, trace dolorous rivers through my sanitised palm, and stuff my scrip with tissues and other essentials. We're all pilgrims now, knees bruised with supplication, offering thanks for our laboured breath as we circle each briefing's newly-minted sins. It's a long way up and I rope myself to friends and strangers alike, leaving two metres of slack in case we fall into each other's arms, a loose rosary lacking a single prayer. At this altitude, there's no one but poets, anxious about influence, and politicians glad-handing their sheep and goats in spite of their own rules. It's the same old story, with nothing new but accents and inflections, its protagonists indistinguishable behind hand-stitched masks. Critics and scholars will one day judge our tales and cartographers may cast shadows of doubt on our unmapped terrain. Over the next rise, or the one after that, is a garden with a pure fountain and a river of dreamless sleep, but it's one step forward and one step back, and the only signs are warnings and prohibitions. Friends long gone pass like cut-out puppets and, as I pinch my fingers, the world shakes with souls ascending to Tier 2, Tier 3, Tier 4, and the tears of a crocodile in an ill-fitting suit.

Oz Hardwick

Thirsty Work

Can this mild waterfall be called
      a waterfall at all? I follow
            clear water flowing over rock
broadening into stairs of water
      flowing over rocks, broadening
            to seating-places, limestone-mild;
knowing there are tripping-places,
      drowning-places, I sit softly
            in flowing water listening
to people singing, walking hard.
      I, who never had the talent
            to improvise, sing a descant.
You were there, friend. And you were there
      in the swimming baths, where ladies
            talked of hip and knee replacements.
You were there, a flash of fuchsia
      when my eyes blacked out, but I kept
            talking till bullying unlooped.
A soft and tricky sacrifice
      phosphoresces up from marshland.
            You are there. You maze me away.
Mountain descending a staircase,
      you appear all plateaus, promise
            amazement, if only
I can stop seeing upside-down,
      seeing everything upside-down.
            Do you want to talk? Here I am.

Vahni Capildeo

On the Verge

We have sewn our own eyes shut, so we don't see the bags of provisions going over the edge. Hordes of us lie, bereave(d of move)ment. We/they lie in half-lit rows of beds—too dim to walk any more—calling out, *Is this Hell?* Burdened, we climb the tiers. The giant sloth emboldens us to run, bearing leaden tons of gravity, away from the rising graphs, the ups and downs, the flat, flat lines. Rats come out of the woodwork but they don't carry plague, just the hope of a cleaner planet. So we race, staying in place, like the Red Queen, in this backwards game of bones. Weeping floods the streets, makes it dangerous to pass; half the roads are closed, the other half deserted. It's like house arrest, we/they say. It's lockdown. It's locking ourselves in with stitches we have applied ourselves, so we don't see the bags of fertiliser thrown over the edge. We don't want our bodies morphed by way of experiment, the way they do it in Hell. We don't want to eat morphed grain. We would rather starve, we/they say. But the ones that don't say, just starve. Who is left to farm when all of us are lying, heavy with boulders, our eyes sewn shut with our own needles, pecking up grain and adding it to the hoards we cover with our own bodies, climbing the tears? Angels appear and we clap them but we/they don't pay for the service.

Amina Alyal

Lockdown Triptych

hellish

the very many dead I could forget
by breakfast that first spring of the lockdown
I spent with you were not a memory yet
I took these little cans of gin round town
to mark the time I wore when she was gone
the face of that lot waking on the ground
in their allotted ring what have I done
it's raining fat and I must heave this bare
shit-pot round a pond while lamps thump on
for keeps and cunting insects everywhere
some scribbler doing his bit to settle scores
I've been there I am there now I'll be there
with always acid tingling in the pores
as my old fingers swell into old claws

purgatorial

the noonday sunshine shining everywhere
        a sunny easter sunday on the stone
white steps of the estate I locked down there

all year now it is easter everyone
        is negative slap happy as I am
on the stone white sunny steps I am far gone

on drink and drunk on wait citalopram
        for what I lost at ten past four perhaps
I grasp an end of my granddaughter's pram

from silver cross and lift it down the steps
        while no one has the other end and I'm
so freaking old I am who no one stops

until they've got to and they do in time
to save the world again in the sunshine

heavenly

the story told above is told below
when taid is there when taid is not I'm taid
the welsh for grandad taids do come and go

like well it writes itself the lawn is wide
with yesterday the story told above
is told below when taid is there when taid

is not the story told is told with love
for taid whose name will never change again
for you my daughter's daughter neighbour of

creation well it writes itself its pen
he was a while the story told above
is on the lips of one remembering when

but she forgets what she was speaking of
and all clink glasses in an olive grove

Glyn Maxwell

Paradiso

High temperature.
The up-line
and the down-line:
mercury in thermometers.

Bedded in broken granite,
concrete sleepers.
Soiled with oil,
receding to infinity.

There is an upright lever,
a manual switch.
You need all your strength.
Pulled down to 45 degrees,
it operates the turnout
to the rusty sidings.

Where the air simmers.
Nothing moves.
Himalayan balsam.
Old Man's beard.

A tiny stand of tansy
feints in the heat.

A greenbottle, still
as a glass hatpin,
sun iridescent
in its greeny golds.

This is forever.
I was expecting my mother
with butter for the bump on
my brow.

But this is forever.

Craig Raine

32

Everything Is Motion

La Gloria di Colui che tutto move,
per l'Universo penetra, e risplende…
—*Paradiso I.1–2*

and shining far below
us bay pulls
tight to ocean that
foundering over
and over pulling back
then climbing itself
again rides its own
rip and listen
           like
trumpets there must be
joy each wave
lifting a head to shout
over and over the rocks
echo they die
too in the roiling
and swimming up
through deep water
           oh
sing unto the Lord
the rolling shanty
of your life nothing
I thought would happen
has yet still spray
carrying light upward
into air loses itself
melts
      quick as Eucharist
as hope
moving in us melts
and streams as through
streaming water ocean

pulls for home in
the bay below and every
thing is glorious
with motion

Fiona Sampson

The Archipelagos

towards a paradiso

    say that somehow you once walked
on the Archipelagos
each one like a half-submerged
turtle in emerald ooze,
that each stride, from one
to the other
pressed each taciturn turtle
down a little—all
turtles being taciturn—
and once your step had passed on
how they bobbed back up,
depressed lightly, un-depressed
with the same taciturn half-smile
really not a smile at all
but a rictus. Your forty-
league boots would flatten dock-leaf,
willow-herb, belladonna, bergamot, brit
and unperceivably the
Archipelagos
themselves, with blissful
unconcern. No tectonic
plate inviolate, no crease,
temporary crease in the
ocean, not straightened out
these are The Straits of Logic,
The Straits of Increase, The Straits
of Sorrow, The Strait of Straights—
they are yours and you fold them
neatly into a known map
and then roll it up.

and so, to the dog-house: once sent here,
hang and wait for a hint of
marsupial or straw,
interchangeable as they are;
by the spider-house
loiter with the Latin-tags
and fully-fused animal smell
   impregnating the air. Stay there.

   the convener of
the Un-Conscious Bias Seminar
was biased towards us
   because we were unconscious.

   everything else is whoops and strained calls
echoic against cool tiles
   and always for the mother, the mother.

   say that you once walked
on the Archipelagos
and that everything furred
or shelled or feathered,
   first blinked, then shuddered.

                              Matthew Caley

Mayday in Ravenna

for Jo Shapcott

and if I were to call to mind that town, Jo,
I'd see us walk again down streets of flowers
looking for Dante, one springtime, years ago,

Sisson in hand and darting through the showers.
Foolish tourists, who nevertheless understood
to make of this journey something that was ours

that words might light a candle in a dark wood
and friendship be a witness to the hours
spent seeking Virgil on our winding road.

Bands played, roses lined the cafés and the bars,
Dante slept, rain fell as we strolled slowly on
under darkening cloud, eyes tilted at the stars.

Maura Dooley

IRELAND

Erin and her Bishop

Nine times down, I walk the frozen lake
      where to fall is to fall through.

Eternally east of me, my heart,
      stopped by snow, feathers my flight.

Conscience is my guide, and constant
      my unfaith in spired holy-huts.

I walk the frozen lake, nine times round,
      where to fail is to fall away.

And then, sounds of this dead world
      carry the wind inside its desolation.

In speech lies our stuttering origins.
      And there is Erin and her *arch* bishop,

stoppering the ice—she grinding
      his bony crown, glubbing clotted-sap,

and him, drivelling, *His Grace*
      is displeased, His Grace is displeased.

When she senses me, she leaves off her frenzy,
      he sold my children, she screeches, spitting

jellied brain, *and those he didn't sell,*
      he starved, and those he didn't starve

he buried in his bowels. Oh foetid burials.
      Her own betrayals are stones

that damn her eyeless sockets,
      and when a tempest fetches

groans to stay her torn mouth,
        she returns to her gnashing.

Beneath my feet, beneath the freeze,
        bodies of ten thousand naked sorrows

bump the ice, hold their infant breath
        as they flow away from Erin and her bishop.

Eleanor Hooker

Nightwalkers

For such pride, here one pays the penalty
—Purgatorio XI.88

We went, hoping to see the pipistrelle,
but hearing a low vibrating rasp, followed that
down the brown squelch of the pine wood
where the old pond had refilled after recent floods.
And there they were, the toads. Almost in standoff,
brinked with desire, the spotted warble of their throats
engorged, the blaze of their backs seeming to rise
in moonlight then drop in the beam of our weak torches.
Soon the whole pond spilled with toads,
toads pairing left and right, the soft pop as they
mounted each other, as nuptial pads gripped
desperate and fast for long strings of eggs to fertilise.

What did they know as they coupled here
where the pond was showing a scrim of oil?
That they'd search next time for a place to spawn
not washed through by slurry or fracked out of mind?
This night, the smell of waterweed drew them down
while we, with our guide, wanted to see some *nature*.
'Of thousands of streamers, few eggs will survive', she says
and tells us to turn right on the spot, to each keep our place
in the mud, and to retrace our steps up through the wood
foot into foot, using the dips we had already made—
so as not to kill too many toads.

Siobhán Campbell

1300

i

I never fitted in that windy place—
but neither did they. A face, a runner
one instant in a frame, a body stuffed
half underground, they twisted
in search of rest like ancients in their beds;
not truly bodies though, yet their unrest
I felt in my own body, the urgent
hungover battering in my head, my lungs
complaining.
              Hunted by twisters and scooped
forward by demons resenting my gaze
as the forge steamed, I did not escape,
I was expelled. The blast knocking me sideways,
then stilled, but the walls, the stairs,
the precipices wanted me gone.

ii: Circle of the Prodigals

I had spent the legacy they earned,
those ancestors that served their time
in the convent and the internment camp
refining the skills they'd studied
in homes of modest, anxious labour, of long hours
gazing at the accounts, overcrowded beds.

I spent it all on the followers of love not war,
who knew where the keys of intoxication were buried;
they dealt in bribes, their lives, their bodies, currency;
the light of dawn saw them returning,
the jewels in their hats far beyond price.
In the middle Sunday of Lent I remember them;

44

they loved as well as I did, but love destroyed them.
They have left me staring long hours at the accounts.

iii

Years ago, far away, in daylight
stronger than summers here,
we sat under the gazebo
and the voices began, their questions
brought out by the light, their explanations
reflecting light as glass flashes.

We sat on the day of the solar eclipse.
It grew a little dark, the birds interrupted their song,
the boy ran for a shaving glass and a sheet.
We watched the moving star so far away
in the dark depth of the house. All
but one remember it, and he will be a guide
when the darkness comes, until the birds
resume their song, as the light grows strong and plain.

Eiléan Ní Chuilleanáin

At Purteen Harbour

basking sharks, docile as seal pups,
harpooned and netted from currachs,

were towed one by one to the fishery
at the slipway. Fathers and sons

sliced off dorsal fins and hacked
through blubber to reach oil-filled livers.

Sweating in burn-house heat,
they shovelled bleeding flesh

into the rendering machine.
They couldn't wash the smell

from their skin, not if they swam
to Inis Gealbhan at the end of every shift.

Year by year the catch grew less,
then disappeared.

But late last April, old men
cheered from the headland, and said,

It was as if they'd been forgiven—
a school of twelve cruised into Keem Bay,

moon tails swishing, fins proud
as yawl sails above the waves.

Jane Clarke

O you who come to this house of pain

in the shallow days of December
in our third lockdown
the end of the strangest year we have lived
the noise of the third wave
falling on us
turning us like stones on the shore
they are reporting thousands
o you who come to this house of pain
watch how you go and whom you trust
these are the dark days

stay home they say
stay together by staying apart
go masked in the streets
we are all unclean
and a year ago we knew nothing
the last carefree Christmas
the sound of children's laughter
the house of joy
watch how you go and whom you trust
these are the dark days

photos of last year
need carbon dating
the archaeology of embrace
a handshake petrified in monochrome
a fossilised smile
the beating of heart on heart
only detectable in distortions
in the earth's magnetic field
watch how you go and whom you trust
these are the dark days

a terrain in 2020 vision
stratified by nightmare
our self-possession lost
among the coffins
leaving Bergamo in army trucks
the sterile neverland of ICU
the battery of hacking coughs
the belling of the pulse oximeter
watch how you go and whom you trust
these are the dark days

smoke blows down the valley
we're close to zero
and the ground is freezing hard
nature is reckless of our pain
the sun reels and the cold moon follows
and spring will follow winter as of yore
the starlings turn and turn
no refuge only less pain
no hope to comfort them
watch whom you trust and how you go
these are the dark days

December 31st

William Wall

Punch Rock

for Kerry Wallace

The only irritant
on this pristine morning
as I sit out sipping
black Tanganda tea
with a hunk of submerged
garden lemon in a hand–
thrown cerulean blue
and white porcelain cup
is the unidentifiable
small brown bird
flitting among emerald
Acacia canopies
sweeping downwards
to a brimming dam.

Joseph Woods

Native Trees

Yesterday she sent me the mountain side,
all pink Flannel flowers and shrubby greens

flowing for miles to the valley, far as
the eye can see; the understory,

a woodland taken root, after wild fires
of last summer reached a pine

at the bottom of the garden, crackled
along the fence through undergrowth

and threatened the house. Down the road
a community fled stifling heat; blinded

by smoke they struggled to breathe;
returned to charred stumps of trees,

that hinterland, a smouldering desert,
a blackened ruin of foul embers

and bitter tears. Now, plants not seen
for years germinate from seed and pollen,

after nestling a lifetime in forest shade,
break dormancy in warm sunlight,

sprout ferny leaves and blooms;
soften the wounded earth with myrtle

and gum saplings, counter human failings
and greed with a wilderness of native

trees, have us dream of the paradise
given; our abundant heaven.

Catherine Phil MacCarthy

The Whisperer

for Martin

Today she woke remembering
an old story—seven wild horses
leaping from a cliff-top,
diving to the ocean
five hundred feet below.

As with the best of all fables, nothing
is as first it seemed—
a story from a woman
so long in the wilderness
five years and five, and five again,
her ritual confiding in the sea
to cast seven old love letters
on horses' backs out into the waves
scattering in all directions, until
they hitched a sea-change north
in the Atlantic drift from Carraigaholt,
Lahinch, Spanish Point, washing up
in some distant archipelago in Scandinavia.
Jumbled signals ionised and crackling
with white noise.

Her lover is a seer, un-showy and modest,
he'd impressed her with persistence, solemn vows, sincerity,
past the brutal father, others:
the passive, the caustic, the neglectful,
the mean of spirit, the casual and selfish
the snivelling and sadistic, the weak and cowardly.
The good. The otherwise committed.
The simply envious.

She was a woman
flinching *ipso facto,*
every time he reached
across another crumpled hotel bed
to touch her face, though
she craved him and though he was kind. Unfailingly so.

He is a whisperer of sorts it seems,
gifted with deciphering
silences, code, encryption,
love, erotic romance from the broken
spaces in between. He believed her.

Divining the familiar, the domestic, the glorious-ordinary,
all life, a shelter, a realm, a province grounded
out of the imagination and echoing in pulse
on pulse, as light across the darkness,
from a tower out at sea,
infinite, tending a beacon blazing
in an open cupola.
Guiding her back. Contented. Of her own accord.

Maria McManus

Of Pure Faith

The maiden, though we hardly knew her, was Kamala Harris,
All Indian and Caribbean island, with dancing stars for eyes.
After the long Purgatorio of unreason we come to this
Intelligent, laughing woman, Attorney General from Paradise.

Frightened still, made nervous by those years of flames,
We reach the verdant riverbank not quite believing: it
Can't be such an easeful transition out of Fascist claims
And Fascist ways. That we escaped before it was too late

Seems now like something written in a book, and written by
A dreamer on too much Napa Chardonnay. O! Believe it!
Believe Hope because Hope can happen. It's no lie
When Reason surfaces. It can happen in the dead quiet

Of a ballot box, the dead quiet where the mob can't come,
Intimidating the downcast, the educated man and woman
Who cower in the side-streets. Here's Dante. Make room
For knowledge. Clear the streets for poetry. A viaticum

Has passed through the darkness, a wafer of pure faith;
And this gentleman beside her, silver haired, full of flaws,
Seems as humane as the flawed can be. It was nearly too late
But we reached the far shore. Of Biden, his fifty dancing stars.

Thomas McCarthy

54

Love

After the Paradiso

There seemed no point in analysing
transcendence
when you took to beach and bar,
imagined paradise, meaning *freedom*

Kusadasi in the 80s,
a circle dance, the soft beat
from an afternoon of heat, and wine,
and more wine, moments and rhythms
febrile as you shuffled, your brown arms
encoiled with his
          Your vision at that time:
to love and be loved, too simple
for any philosopher, theologian, or the poet
who insists we cannot know that which creates
un-knowing
blows you sweetly towards the empyrean,
seen in childhood. 'So, mother,
are there angels in that place?'
Yes, she replies, filling your head
with choices like wing colour: *anything you*
desire, crimsons, golds, silvers, halcyons,
greens, and sparkle too for the cherubic type.
'You go there to praise God,' she continues,
'nothing else.' Which isn't bothersome,
prayer & praise, all else laid on,
no division of hours, minutes,
sweet moments of not quite knowing
the unknowable

This, your place—child, girl,
woman—what you have always known,
your place

in a blue cosmos the Limbourg Brothers
would later borrow
your place in empyrean space
praise   praise   praise
for what you never knew but always sensed,
and now you, you, you, released and wingèd,
o mother, rise up through poetry,
vocal chords vibrating, tongue unsprung
at last, your pure heart distilled by joy

Mary O'Donnell

UNITED STATES OF AMERICA

The Pile

It seemed to happen then for all at once—
not *to* but *for*, a prognosis, a gift
none could refuse though many would renounce
as coruscating dust continued to drift

    and lodge particulates in eye and lung.
    Some watchers couldn't help trembling,

so they turned to glance around instead
at granite faces gaping at the scene.
Some stared at the ground where their shadows shed.
A newspaper. A door. A flashing screen.

    It happened as a chronic disenthralling—
    it happens still for those who can't look long

at images of charred concrete or beam,
for those who, even as it happened, knew
that day would inform whoever they became
when the pile was cleared. None are those people now

    who searched steel spandrels for the ones who'd flung
    their bodies from so high it looked like flying.

Some stalked hospitals. Some set down flowers,
carnations wrapped in crinkled cellophane,
where others had taped *Have You Seen Me* fliers.
Some tried to reach the missing on the phone.

    Some held the hands of strangers stopped along
    the Armory fence, the wind rattling.

This is who they were, an *us*, those who stayed
for a month, a week, a few days at least,

before the searing polymer reek gave way
to low-tide odors wafting from the east.

   Some drove home then, staying in their lane,
    to mortgaged rooms they'd spent a life filling.

Some floundered in a kind of undertow
dragging them back to those same photographs
they peered at until they didn't know
what was true. Some stifled rueful laughs,

   wading through the day's clamor and clang
    as through beached cargo or a stone dome falling.

Some walked away from fires blazing for weeks
below the streets, a smoldering cascade
that burned sunk joists and pilings down like wicks.
Some squinted at the blue that absence made,

   and felt unequal to the rubble's longing
    to be ash, the brackish river's seaward lunge.

Brian Brodeur

Still, Above Grass

Or going for a walk after reading Dante

Francesca's memory has one small flaw:
when her affair with Paolo goes astray,
she fails to note he's her brother-in-law.

Study what they did and not what they say.
Just following orders, Eichmann made clear.
Hell's much more crowded since Dante's day.

ARBEIT MACHT FREI—death's taunt austere—
is forged in plain font on the gates of Hell:
Abandon all hope ye who enter here.

The monatto signals his ankle bell,
dragging corpses to graves with hands worked raw,
and air tainted with a rancid-sweet smell.

Drained from the descent through Hell's gaping maw,
I long for earth's light, imperfectly flawed.

Cindy Frenkel

Level Six (Man, It's a Hot One)

Every soul
sorry
with sores

From the midday sun   matches
sear skin   erupt
nerves

Every sore
weeps yellow
tears

Each nerve
a tentacle
wav(er)ing

What's worse?
tearing skin
or shredded flesh

Electric bolts
take the left calf
muscle for a midnight

Flesh zinging like
digits jammed
in a socket

jolt. Is it meant to be
like a roof dropping
shingles singly?

Water draining
from blisters
doesn't quench.

Kimberly K. Williams

Mr Blanquito in Hell

John Wannamaker was my prophet. His store
in Philadelphia had a pipe organ as big
as any cathedral's. 'The store is an Easter Egg,'

he wrote. His ads made his merchandise seem
like wondrous accessories of the Resurrection.
At Christmas, he festooned his store with model

church spires, stained glass windows, & stars.
I worked as Creative Director for Hexman
& Shafton, an ad agency. Once, we fought

over what to rename our agency with its
new offices in Brooklyn, Sydney, & London.
Thinking of St Wannamaker—how gladly

we mistake goods for goodness—I suggested
'The Cathedral of St Randy the Insatiable.'
The senior partners were not amused,

& they chose 'Millennial Communications
Company.' I made our new logo—MC^2—as if
we were part of a brilliant equation, although

we were merely engineers of desire & self-
gratification. Virgil explained to Dante that
some souls are so corrupt they fall to hell

even before their bodies have died. I know
I probably fell into the eighth circle already,
along with Pope Boniface, Donald Trump,

many US senators, & my colleagues.
I sometimes recall my grandmother, slipping
on her white gloves—all her lady-friends wore

white gloves to church—as if desire & prayers needed
special handling. I wonder what happened
to the boy I was, who knelt beside her to light

votive candles. After college, I wandered across
Europe & ran out of money in Paris. I slept
a few nights at Shakespeare & Company

in exchange for restocking books & doing
odd jobs. I wish I could say it was romantic,
but I was miserable. The soles of my shoes

were peeling away, & from the bookstore's
little bed, I picked up a few battalions of lice.
One afternoon, I took my hunger & vermin

to Notre Dame, to sit in the sacred light
of the great rose windows. I prayed,
not for my grandmother, not for heaven—

I prayed that I would never be this poor
ever again—which is really an anti-prayer.
Not long after that, I began my career

as a strip-miner of the dearest vistas
of your unconscious. You know that song
you loved as a teenager, the one you heard

when you & your love made love
in the back seat of your car
for the first time? I bought the rights

to that song & then applied it to a million
TV ads for a chain of awful restaurants.
I'm the guy who put luxury cars with big

red bows in the driveways of commercials
at Christmas time. Because you're worth it.
Because you deserve a break today, because

the best or nothing. The portals of avarice
are as near as your mobile phone, your TV,
your google-search. There's no chance

for a rose window to cast the prevailing light
when commerce has portals everywhere.
We want more & fear others have more than us.

'We're better than this,' the new President says.
I worry he is wrong. We stoked these fires as if
we cherished them—but how empty their heat.

D.W. Fenza

Altarpiece

This Place

—First fall day, the first real day of fall,
and there will be another after that.

—Firm footing gave the maker of the world
to man and woman, once they settled down.
Almost at once ground shifted underfoot.

—This place is not so bad. It's not so bad.
We rode here on the eon and the instant
and probability's our one clairvoyance.

—Why do we feel so lost among these trees?

—Don't think about it but let muscle memory
ease the descent. The occasion's gravity
appears in green grime under fingernails
and scales the damage done by sun to scalp.

—Where were we? Oh, once upon a time,
gray drizzling overcast, bright yellow gingkos,
the first day that was purely an autumn day,
and in tomorrow's forecast, brilliant sunshine
like a folktale forestalling ugly death.

—But we're not gonna die tomorrow yet.
We'll wait to see the peak of fading color.

—How honest can it be to remain sane?

—They only lasted six hours in the garden.

The Other Place

Down where the murderer and thief,
the liar, the ruiner of childhood,
the sinner who's a cutthroat from the womb,
the banger, bomber, roller-out of hangars—
hang out, it's all a lot more colorful.
Up here the mountain sides you have to cling to,
monochrome and sheer, too close for comfort,
keep you focused on getting on with it.

Take envy, Good Lord! It's already painful,
wanting this one's heart, that one's rifle scope,
this one's loving viewpoint, that one's book review,
like trying to fill a trophy room with dog doo.
With both eyes woven shut, all you can see
is the lining of your skull's own nooks and crannies.

Apparently a purging makes you lighter,
though I have heard the bitter aftertaste
turns down the corners of your mouth forever,
and burning off the fat can waste your heart.
Wanting to have that boyish girlish figure,
eating and gagging up the dog's dinner,
will help you let it out and make it better.

But in the other place no one gets better.

That Place

At last, at last, up here you can be good,
and over there and under, all around,
the way you always wanted but forgot.
And yet and yet desire still exists.
Not everybody's looking up at God,
that waterlily in the pond of heaven.
Some shimmy and some shine, and some cavort,
enjoying one another bathed in grace.
The argument is amazingly familiar:
if nature were allowed to take its course
and it was understood, its basic goodness
would fit us in the element made for us,
if only we would do what we were told,
not by our parents, who probably didn't listen,
but by our hearts and minds and willing members
as easily as touching a finger to your nose.
Some may enjoy more radiance than others
but everybody gets the same sunshine,
apportioned to the genius of their skill.
That one that you were always meant to be,
dogeared or foxed or sun-bleached on a shelf,
will bind you, soul and body, to yourself.

Mark Jarman

Comedy

1. Where you go for the company, not the climate

My grandmother used to call it, in the state
Where she retired to watch the sunset, over
-the-yard-arm whisky in her left hand, in her right
A cube of Wisconsin cheese. And later, we toured

The supermarket lot in her Nova, my Virgil
Gossiping about the dead—all her old circle
Wicked-fast company like her. She cornered
Hard, cocking an eye for a cart to lean on

And push, like every day, into the store, all
The time speculating like an old Italian which long
-dead beaux and rivals would have ended

Where, given what chores for their errors. Where
She landed I haven't nerve to wonder.
I only wish her the best in conversation.

2. The Late Middle

Who knew this would be so much work?
Dash through a curtain of fire, rinse,
Repeat. I thought I'd just have to wait,
Swinging my foot and tapping the table, not

Dash through curtains of fire. Rinse
Then wire my eyes shut so they can't devour
Someone's Manolo swinging, jeweled fingers tapping
A lyric I can't get out of my head. It makes me

Want to wire my ears shut. Already, I can't see
Through the smoke rings I blow
Trying to clear my head, that make me
Want to flip my lid, or just lie down. What with

All the smoke I have to blow
I'm too busy huffing around to chat
Or let off steam or have a lie-down. Given
Everything here takes its own sweet time

I'm too busy counting down to chat;
And if I love in excess the world's offerings—
Its sweets, its good time—what I take
Is good to have but not to want,

Or want whatever too much is. All earth offers
Binds me to it and makes me dust.
What is good: to have, but not to want;
All is good to have, except desire

Binds me to it. If dust makes flesh,
Fruit hangs out of reach. What makes dust?
Good to have but not desire to get
The mouth around—everything. Dangle

Out of reach the dust-made fruit,
The body's fruits the poets sing to get
Their mouths around: every dang thing
I should not have touched. Wanting

Them, I mouthed them into song. Get,
Repeat. I thought I'd mostly have to wait,
Trying not to touch what I could reach.
Who knew that would be so much work?

3. As usual, I was going to skip Paradise,

Famously changeless and full of instruction,
When near over the eaves rough-danced
The pair of Cooper's hawks keeping house
Nearby—lofting over the canyon

Half-tumbling up and up to get at each other,
Touching wings and breasts, holding talons
And beaks away from tender bellies,
Deploying rough-body caress in dalliance

As they rose. If later they light from wilderness
Of air, if sun, wind, and sinew bear
Their hollow bones into summer, if the nest

They line with their own breast-down
Holds, chicks will hatch and call, fledge
And also fly. It will happen here.

Katharine Coles

Slow Pilgrim

—all manner of thing shall be well

Ἀδης [Hades]

Ah, the gates to hell? Just here
behind my eyes. And yes, the gates
remain full open, even as night
descends, and I close my eyes, which
serves only to begin a fresh
descent. Have a look. Hell turns out
to be a region of the gut.
Καρδιά? Νους? Whatever. Close enough.
The region of that intellective
ache I surely had suspected
long before this drop into the Dis.
Every wretched denizen
turns out to be my own creation,
and while each is singularly
wretched, my array of grim
malefactors shares a common
complaint—that each was somehow
justifiable, that none was
ever free to be otherwise.
I want to believe them, but I
am not alone, and—given that
I am not alone—I know far
better than to take their word
for anything, especially
for anything so self-serving as
excuse. We are not alone. Truth
stands even here among us, Truth
Himself remains just here, attentive
and immovable within my νους.
And He will surely not agree
to acquiesce to my sad fictions.

Καθαρτήριο [Purgatory]

And thus begins, as well, the long
recuperative endeavor,
this harrowing of hell, this late
repair of my disparate
constituents, late cure of my
long belovèd illness. Do I
want to be healed? Let's say I do,
at least today. For the moment,
then, I choose to face Himself,
and in that moment the chagrin
is frankly searing, so I turn
away—though if you *must* know,
one cannot quite turn away, not
any longer. He proves manifestly
present, everywhere. Every angle
proves face-to-face, and so the sear
continues, intermittently
acute, intermittently a bit
diminished, but always keen
to cauterize the wound, the several
cherished wounds. And always, with the sear,
the acrid scent, the smoke, the odd
sense of relief—that finally
I am maybe getting somewhere.

Παράδεισος [Paradise]

Somewhere turns out to be precisely
where I have always stood, or sat,
or languished unawares. The difference,
now, is that my eyes are open.
And shame or fear or nagging
culpability has been eclipsed
by...what? Willingness? Concurrence?
I would call it a late-recovered
sympathy with *what is*, a desire
to see *what is*, and to apprehend
its comeliness. It appears, here,
at the center of all things—here,
at the center of myself—as
a font, a flower, a blossoming
excess, which I am finally
awake enough to now receive.

Scott Cairns

Beatrice in Exile

What purgatory is, is what
it's not: scorching repetition
refracting in this fluted glass,

me, Beatrice, its greedy fire
releasing sudden cardamom,
like the venial's smoky spice.

Twenty-five years. Moved in place,
I've scribed a life, not what you bought,
unassimilated, but my own.

Ambition masquerades as flaw.
Animal wrath's dark running
ran out into a howl one night,

at dawn, almost subsiding.
As a cat, safe behind a screen,
outside spies an undomestic

litheness in the light fog, alert
and rising into memory,
postprandial. We ascended,

our brilliant, drunken repartee
litter up the subway's stair,
word by word, onto 23rd Street.

*

In my fashionable shades, perfect
for a worldly Empyrean,
I read Dido's submission

to the genius of your control
of her passion to master your own.
I smile. My spirit, unpublished,

a rose between foxed pages,
won't allow the book to close.
There's still a linger of what it is

not to pass beyond the human,
its little bit of rot, its sillage
and hypervigilance.

In time, astronomical,
as in fantasy, or high tide,
I descry justice. Vision's uplift

is its idiom, actions bad—and
not so awful—rehabbed, unstylish,
my vernacular's tumbled gems.

Janet Sylvester

To Dante, Seven Hundred Years On

Tongue-tied, I'll let your words start me off:
amor mi mosse, che mi fa parlare;
I've wanted to write them all my life

and you might like to hear their echoes carry
unbroken over seven hundred years,
even if you'd balk at their trajectory

through my unsuitable, if fervent, ears.
Unless you've mellowed in Paradise.
Or maybe you're not there yet, still need prayers

(from the living, this time) to gain release
from Purgatory's lowest terrace (Pride).
I'd volunteer, but for your purposes

am fairly certain my prayer's no good.
The *love* that *moved me* and *makes me speak*
is for your poem, Dante, not your God.

You've failed with me. I'm still a heretic.
But it's hard to imagine any poet
making even mild doctrine stick;

lyric tends to weave a strand of doubt
into anything resembling an assertion,
to prime and animate its opposite.

For all your *Commedia*'s religion,
its bribes, its threats, its acrid discipline,
it can't help bearing out that to be human

is to flounder in the long standoff with sin.
You're most affecting when you're full of pity
and probably at your most genuine

succumbing to your own humanity,
colonizing each circle of hell
with loathed archrivals from your native city,

their names now only known to us at all
by way of your relentless condemnation.
Your own punishment—a life in exile—

seems inconsequential by comparison,
especially in your final stopping place
(who'd imagine bits of glass and stone

could be so flexible, so full of grace?),
each pieced-together laurel, peacock, palm,
lily, ripple of water, blade of grass

from that dreaming instant, Byzantium,
a ready portal to the paradise
you entered daily in your triple rhyme,

mapping out a detailed route for us.
Forgive me, Dante. I'm not ungrateful,
but I can't follow, gorgeous as it is;

I prefer remorse, exertion, struggle
to even the most exquisite stasis,
rarely read past *Purgatory* and *Hell*

(piety's less riveting than pathos).
At least, that's my position in *this* life
which I suspect's the only one there is.

And it does have marvels. You yourself
were raised among them, your native city
spilling over—even then—with proof

of purely earthbound immortality.
Now, it adorns itself with the attention
(to Ponte Vecchio, Arno, baptistery ...)

you lavished on it, turning homespun Tuscan
into high Italian, your words on show
everywhere in Florence etched in stone.

Even at my bus stop in Galluzzo
(my dear friend lives there; it's where I stay)—
e al Galluzzo e a Trespiano—

here you are!—*aver vostro confine* ...
Galluzzo marks that border even now;
piazza, streets and houses still give way

to olive groves and vineyards, the very view
that saw you off on any southward journey.
Perhaps it's from this very spot that you

had your *villan* look *down across the valley*
as fireflies caroused and burned all night
di tante fiamme tutta resplendea

(of all your detours, long my favorite).
Now, there's no *villan.* It's only me,
the fireflies less copious, less bright.

Dare I invoke you, when it's *only me?*
Only me, Dante, *and the broken light.*

Jacqueline Osherow

Landscape: Full Emptiness

The lake is frozen under snow
and winter's slanted light burns low.
The only sound's the testy caw
and wing flap of a single crow.

Prints around the lake's edge draw
the shapes of wing or tail or paw
that tell us we are not alone
but share in mortal nature's law.

Each single flake of snow that's flown
and landed where the wind has blown
now shines its tiny brilliant light,
burnishing tree and drift and stone.

Full emptiness is deep and bright,
river of form and eye and sight—
gift of wave and drift and flight,
wave and wind and drift and flight.

Sidney Wade

AUSTRALIA

Hiroshima Triptych

Relics of Hiroshima

Now, I'm sorry that those things had to happen, but they did, and I don't have any sympathy today because of it. I've never had a sleepless night (Applause)

Hiroshima is burning. The bright bulb on the belly of the plane explodes over the city in red-heat. I've heard the sound of detonation secondhand, the low-pitched buzzing of slow bees in a hive. I've seen nuclear shadows etched on sidewalks; the shape of a woman with a walking stick bleached onto the stairs of the bank. From the plane, they see the landscape as a smudged charcoal drawing; they watch the city fall to ashes. By the side of the road, there's a woman and her baby, still attached by the umbilical cord. The plane is already heading home.

If Dante had been with us on the plane, he would have been terrified.

Time is like a keloid that keeps returning. Black rain stripes white walls in inky watercolour. We see twisted metal and debris, a stack of fused teacups— fragments of lives that persevere. The hibakusha sobs as he holds up his sister's school shirt. It trembles like a flag.

Hiroshima is for Lovers

Nothing happened. Forget that I kissed you in Hiroshima. Leave behind our hot silences and your shoulder nestling against mine on the blue streetcar circling the city. Remember that your body is marked by others' narratives and their stories don't belong on my lips. Your wife is waiting at the hotel bar with a bottle of cold, white wine and an empty glass and she will take the streetcar with you tomorrow. // Everything happened. In your hotel room, you stretched my arms above my head and placed my palms on the window. From behind, you pressed me against the glass, like a specimen. I saw the steel skeleton of the A-bomb dome against the blue sky. I tried to speak but my words slipped down the Ōta River and into the Seto Inland Sea. We stood on the Aioi bridge and I imagined its T shape as a ventricle, and you its beating heart.

Shrine Island

At high tide, the torii gate floats in the Seto Inland Sea, its vermilion camphor and cedar posts rising from the water in a shock of neon. I ask you to take my photo while I stand on the flat rock in a pink velour mini skirt—and years later it looks like a prayer. We walk to *Kakiya* and I eat too many oysters, tucking their salty creaminess into my cheeks. Later, Sika deer follow you to the ferry, a convoy of spotted bodies and expressive eyes. Outside the village the island is mostly wilderness. Beyond the radiation zone, glassy particles on the shore betray its proximity to Hiroshima. As misty twilight settles over Miyajima, you open the window and we make love on an unmade bed in the Hiroshima Prince hotel; our limbs are a blue-tinted vanishing point.

Cassandra Atherton

For Dante and All Conjurers

The Poet's Lake

And saw before and underneath my feet
A lake, whose frozen surface liker seem'd
To glass than water...
—Inferno XXXII.23-25

A mirror then—so did you see your face?
As your feet burned on ice and shivering,
You saw those two locked tight in an embrace.
One with teeth on the other's skull, lusting
To fracture bone and all that lie beneath,
The murder and the treachery, the rage
Both ice and fire, so you could barely breathe.
Poet, this is your history, each page.
Your amygdala, that little almond
As fired up in your skull as in those two
That cut you once. How then to miss the bond
With those into eternal hell you threw?

Write them underneath your feet clean and whole?
But this ice burns from sole to scalp to soul.

The Place Beneath

There is a place beneath,
From Belzebub as distant, as extends
The vaulted tomb, discover'd not by sight,
—Inferno XXXIV.121-123

But he is there because you put him there,
You, deft kingmaker, who could unseat king
After king, make king after king with care
Of heart and will that drive your pen to sing
Of exploits fake or true but truer made

89

By trick of light, or double-face or phrase
To make the kill. For story is your trade
And lives are players in your spiral maze.
But he is there because you put him there,
That king who'll never want to leave or die.
How evict him now? Your story is his air,
Your maze, his might; your phrase, his vilest lie.

Purgatory's the place beneath his throne
Where you can plot unseating Satan's own.

The Poet's Sandal

> 'Look how thou walkest. Take
> Good heed, thy soles do tread not on the heads
> Of thy poor brethren.'
> —*Inferno XXXII.20-22*

What privilege to descend into hell,
Rise to paradise then return to earth
To write. Thank god, you're safely back and well.
Arbiter of dark and light, hurt and mirth,
Your metre calculates how far and deep
The fall, and how stygian the pit, how damned
The villains on these pages—how you weep
For all pinned down by righteous pen in hand.
But it's fate: only the poet can rise
After descent, enlightened. By his fire,
He alone is purged from the witnessed strife,
Eyes clearer, ears purer, heart free of ire.

Though there's a bit of bone, a hair or two
Caught on his sandal—at least, no one knew.

Merlinda Bobis

Purgatory

I can't sleep here,
in this curve of the East Baines River—
too much blood on the ground,
and my campfire throws a mottled light
over mulga, burnishing insects,
and filling this changeling night with forms.

When it's humid like this,
sound travels.

Crocodiles barking
in the creek behind the van park, somewhere
a car radio plays Bowie:
> *for we're like creatures of the wind,*
> *and wild,*
> *wild is the wind.*

On these banks, boabs
hold stars between their fingers
like splintered bone—
their torsos are globes, carved
with images of snakes and the names
of those shot while dancing ceremony,
on a night just like this, a night split
by rifles—the first crack
erupts the egrets
from the river's still surface.

A century is nothing for boabs.

These roots remember
the warm weight
of babies, pushed by their mothers
into blackness and the living smell of mud—
how they slipped

through water's dark like creatures
of wind and wild is
my breath

becomes the sound of water hissing
through roots, snakes carved
in a boab's skin,
like the snake that comes to me in dreams
speaking her language of coagulants,
blood venom, neurotoxins.

Lightning eddies through the interior of clouds—
a dangerous lightning,
opening like wings
or branching nerves—and in its light,
all those drowned babies are gliding
above the river,
their slow heads turning
to hold me, in their savage windburned gaze.

Time to go.

I wake the dog, upend a billycan on the fire.
A few minutes to pack the ute, and we drive east
into landscape cloaked in Witchetty—
and the boabs follow,
burning their way out of form.
I carry them as sparks in my iris,
in the familiar sea-green lights of the dash,
as min-min racing beside the road.

One eye on the rear-view mirror,
East Baines River vanishes
into the reach of mountains.
The last boab
is a great, dark octopus

silhouetted against stars.
A bellbird drops from its branches as we pass,
arcing noiselessly into headlights,
its western wing,
its wild and shining eye.

Judith Crispin

Envy

(Purgatory: The Second Terrace)

It was predictable enough
    that couples walking arm in arm
        would have multiplied.

        And of course the love scenes in movies
           are more frequent than before.

And I've noticed there are
    more recipes impossible
      to downsize
        from two serves to one:

        (a quarter of a pinch
           is an eighth of almost nothing.
             And how do you measure
                half an egg, anyway?).

And then there is the mouth guard
    you once wore on your upper teeth
      to protect them from your nighttime grinding.

        How it sits unused on my bedside table
           in its case. How I've tried to embrace

what we have in common, both of us now
    deprived of your mouth in the dark.

      But I can't help coveting
        how it holds, as I do not hold
           the indisputable archaeology of you;

           those tear-shaped indents in their
              half-moon runnel

where at times, when you clamped down hard in dreams
          and broke through the moulded barrier altogether,

             pinpricks of light are visible
                like some peek-a-boo
                   of a new galaxy where dentine
                      and thermoplastics under pressure
                         give birth to incisor stars.

But your mouthguard's not Universal. It's useless
      for anyone but you. Used up, discarded.
                Devoted forever
                  to the shape of your upper jaw.

           A relic, a vessel, a dental record
                  to identify the dead,
                      that's all.

But despite all the biting, the possession and the ruin,
      how much it would have been worth it
                to have known you from the inside out
                   like that.

Judy Johnson

Confession, New Year's Eve 2020

A five minute glitch in the fireworks.
I'd risen from my coma,
climbed a mountain, then promptly
fell in love again
but somehow less disorderly.

Then in scented time-zones of recall I dozed
for years and re-played our every spectacle
—the harbour parties, the all-day-drinking,
the seductions in a kitchen of a large
imposing villa.

Oh pride.
No cast iron balcony could take our weight.
Reputation outgrew our wings.
With the adulation blues again

we date stamped
our lyrics and named the territory:
River, Graveyard, Courland Penders.

11:57 New Year's Eve.
No call for ceremony, subs, flybuys.

We rose from our sickbeds
and went from shed to chateau in the bush.
We went to where the road runs out,

to where our poems
outlasted the bush.
And the crowd anticipated
the lights, the fire.
The spectacle for us.
The gift was never-ending forgiveness and light
and the purest intoxicants.

Freshly bathed and dressed
for the grand opening
of the hippest joint in town
we waited for the Boss to cut the ribbon

re-birthed into higher office,
to Authority now on the 22nd floor,
licensed by the beauty industry
that had hiked up the power
with freebies we could not refuse.

Jetting into permanence, the VIPs of Forever,
the paintwork, the one and only colour
of everlasting life.

We paid for it and banked our sins, my pride!
From childhood's verdant priced-out north,
to exile's fall in Newtown dump!
I had stolen books, not cars.
I lied to my father etc. ...
My apotheosis there.

One bridge, one memory.
Don't look back.
One night of rainbows is enough.

Adam Aitken

Mary in the Gardens of the Sun

You had some really crazy ideas, Dante. Heaven split up into layers, saved souls ranked in order of goodness, and Mary mother-of-Jesus popping up with flowers everywhere. That Beatrice? How could you *think* that such a know-it-all would make the hereafter appealing? Add in some casual anti-Semitism, some one-eyed praise of Rome, some glowing self-promotion, and I am ready to toss you down to the eighth circle of hell.

But Mary in the gardens of the sun, she speaks to me. God might give me the grace to find connection. Who Doesn't Search for Answers? Who Doesn't Wrestle With the Word for Meaning?

I turn in my smug little bubble. So easy to condemn, so hard to love.

I let your longings pierce me

and pluck the flower that shivers like a star. It shrinks into itself—the smallest seed of light, ready to take me to warp-speed. I let myself look up.

Miriam Wei Wei Lo

Concatenation

...I stay on in doubt with yes and no
dividing all my heart to hope and fear.
—*Inferno VIII.107-108*

To hell with it, let's start our great adventure—
though I was happy being freedom's bride.
When you say *stay the night*, I hear *indenture*.

You say it, though, and all gates spring aside.
The rampart's gone, defence's habits wrecked.
We smiled and said *let's just be friends.* We lied.

Hearts' adding-up I'm sure we can perfect,
though calculation doesn't play a part.
We've done subtraction, mastered retrospect.

With yes and no dividing all my heart
I'm all cut up. I failed to learn my tables.
Freedom says *she* gave me all my art—

wants alimony, makes me pay the bills.
Her jealous rage is hard for me to parse.
Yet there you are with all your sparks and cables.

We're sutures, goose bumps, newsflash, love-crumbs, scars.
We're linkage, bruises, terza rima

                                  stars.

Felicity Plunkett

'A man in a face mask crosses London Bridge'

(photo caption, The Age, *17/10/20)*

As he walks, he rehearses a verse from Dante he decided
he must quote in the original. '*Nessun maggior dolore ...*'
(one phrase at a time): There is no greater sorrow ... The Eye
ogles him across the Thames. 'What's up?' he says, out loud.
No-one to hear him on the deserted bridge. He stumbles, steps
on a memory a dozen months old—the innocent, prior past.
He counts his blessings on a fistful of digits, enumerates
those grim joys and compensations that permit us to carry on.

'... *che ricordarsi del tempo felice ...*' Yes, it hurts to recall
their happy times, when the future's shut. Tonight she'll
advise on Skype that she has left him—or if she lacks courage
even for that, she'll send a WhatsApp or some insipid text.
This is the twenty-first century, after all—twenty-first year!
So much for 20/20 vision. He wonders who the novel lover is,
knows only that they met at a book launch. A poet, of course.
She hasn't mentioned a name, just that 'her work has been
an epiphany': that's when the first blow fell—in bed!—
while they were pigging out on the 'fake' US election. Well,
unlike the President, he has no perverse desire to hang around.

'... *nella miseria.*' It hurts; but already he forgives her, casts
his misery on the black ink below. The river forgives everything.
Who said that? Not old Herakleitos, though the sentiment's apt.
Not Alighieri—yet wasn't Lethe's mask a kind of forgiveness?
He lifts his hatch to scratch at his nose, inhales the twilit air,
so crystal pure. Tries to guess Frannie's comeback to his quote,
pretty sure he's got the verse down pat. Over and over it reads
his lips, settles on the desktop of his thoughts—somewhat,
he muses, like one of those virtual backdrops in Zoom.

Alex Skovron

Alcatraz

1. Robert Stroud (Hell)

You are bashed by your father; your mother can't protect you. He knocks her arms aside and strikes her, throwing you to the ground and kicking your legs. He forces you to kneel, tying you to a table with a strap. Ridiculing your speech, he exaggerates your failures—words like clubs a guard might carry. Later someone speaks of childhood's innocence. You're puzzled by what they mean—unless it's grovelling on the floor; unless it's dabbing your mother's swollen face. You leave when you're old enough and try to find another way of living, killing a man who attacks the prostitute you've pimped but care for. As you pull the trigger, your father's face rises from the floor.

2. Birdman (Purgatory)

You're in language's cage, shouting at a guard about 'rights'—but, in this orbit, even your best words won't open the world. 'I love you' improbably excavates the past: you're three years old; your mother grasps your arm; your drunk father throws you to the ground again. Words open in the form of a screaming mouth and, like a modern Jonah, you're consumed. Yet, when you find three injured sparrows in the prison yard, you have access to pity, beginning to breed canaries, feeling their pulsing bodies in your hands. You scan the dictionary for meanings in which to dress your birds and, as words march past, they suggest that language's whine of failure may be mitigated—like Siren songs, their sound appeals like 'freedom'. You publish books. One day you imagine yourself as Icarus, climbing the unquantifiable blue.

3. Death (Paradise)

The birds multiply until there are thousands. You're carried by them—as if floating on an enormous yellow cloud; you play chess against the angels and win, having finally mastered the Queen's Gambit. Your anger dissipates as if in splashes of boiling blood. You cross chasms as dreamscapes, seeing whips, excrement and fire. Your eyes become cloudy, even though you fail to cry. You pass impossible concepts, which you don't remember, and see circles expressing other circles, like a complex mathematics. Your mother looks at you again as if she believes you; your father is under your heel, yet you immediately release him. Nine of the birds are feeding from your hands.

Paul Hetherington

101

Beata

In autumn sunshine, I walk up from the beach,
wave at Belinda, my barber, then the barista boys
at Café Crumb. I go on past the pizza joint on the corner—
its notice in the window: *Apologies we will be closed*
Friday to Monday. Our son Andrew is getting married.
Up Crag Road to the junction with Ocean Street,
turn left into Wattle Crescent and along to our place.
Home, I walk up the stairs into the open-plan light,
look out to sea, the sandy crescent I've just strolled,
there's maybe a sail in sight or motor-boat scoring bubbles
across the blue towards the wooded farther shore,
the uneven line of the purple mountain backdrop.
Is that some weather coming in, I say.
Not forecast for a while yet, you reply.
Then we sit on the deck in the warmth,
above the flourishing garden you've made
with its berries, fruit trees, vegetables,
its roses for remembrance, flowers for joy.
And if six o'clock should come by, I'll say,
Champagne or Chardonnay? Or maybe I'll have a beer.
We'll sit and sip our drinks, and one of us
will say how blessed are we? Chinking glasses,
we know some who would scoff: *sentimental*
or *too simple* or some other argument
for strangulation of all delight; we'll smile
for a moment, try to forget the venal world
and banish the fear this loving place,
our little piece of paradise,
depends on someone else's hell.

Adrian Caesar

SINGAPORE

Queer Filth Infernal

unbelievable, unceasing,
irresistible, unignorable,
in these negatives I only
ghost my hands over
the unknowable shape
of what you are.

love last, love lost;
in this blatant mirage
only one can speak
figures you'd come
for me anyway my
gothic poet laureate
candescent ex fucking your
unctuous glossy fingers

into my parting desert dune
reading murder blackfeather poetry
in this circle dirty is a city
and my fey words reach you
before running in labyrinthine
thicknesses. a wailing, a
good time, she who is called

Incontinence slavering over
us who've made our vows
and burn them in the ash.

my love, sodom, widen
each pouting sphincter
of my hidden wisdom.
grant the caplet teeth
my salvation with your
crown of mud and suckling

gift. your godhead, torn
asunder,

a defiant *kiap*ping of
my thighs, between your
thighs. came down
to the river styx and all
we saw was a wedding
boat, charon's nickel tongue
another rusted openmouth
kiss, bleeding me out

your achilles heel I have
grasped naked o never
let us be those inheriting

the yoke of those who
never lived and can
never die

Marylyn Tan

Astray

'A monk meditating in a forest in Maharashtra
dies in a leopard attack.'

what gently

before our own rude rebirths—
cadavers blotting back into selfsame soil,
    or where I live, uncoiled into ash.

some say the journey is the same.
    to abrogate, proselytise, pulp
            our brain coppices into neat slats.

sometimes at thirty-five we want to feel
that phenomenally opaque curiosity
    of horror-movie characters

& follow our leopards, lions & she-wolves
into our sanctuary, that rabid pastoral
    glitch where puddles lie

iridised with tender oily moonlight.
    lately it is all picket lines set up by
            proud commercial gulls.

all are punished. still we intrude, forsake,
    sin gratefully under the stars, who make
        small circles in the still & soaring dark.

Jerome Lim

From our parents

'*Ara vos prec, per aquella valor*
que vos guida al som de l'escalina,
sovenha vos a temps de ma dolor.'
Poi s'ascose nel foco che li affina.
  —*Purgatorio XXVI.140–48*

Thus have I heard, from our parents
and their parents, the terse remembrance
of their childhoods, their adulthoods,
no full stories, only lessons, things we should

follow or avoid—
to marry, raise up children, stay employed,
more aphorism than memory,
recalling extinct sufferings, every

word sounding like a cliché or an undeserved
scolding. I was loved
in excess, as many children are.
Having received, I demanded more,

not knowing until it is nearly
time for me to love in return, how costly
love can be.
The toll is paid in time, presence, the body

and its work. Was it worth it at all
to raise one who has declined so much of the toll
as I? I am grown, they have little to show
for it. Their stairways climbed, we only know

the old pattern of their sayings: they confide
their past regrets. Their present pain, they hide.
And of the future they won't see, they trust,
wholly fulfilled in us.

Bryan Cheong

Gluttony is no sin in Singapore

Our national sport is eating
or thinking about the next place
to eat, or posting food porn

on our social media accounts.
Gluttony is only a sin in Singapore
if you get fat or sick from it.

But if you don't, please finish everything
you ordered, because wasting food
is the greater sin, and don't you know

that every grain of rice you didn't finish
is a pimple boil
on your future spouse's face?

Gluttony is good
for the economy
and easy to police, or purge

and what's good
for the economy
is good for the country

as long as you don't get sick—
this is no country for the old
and sick—it's too expensive.

We like our old sleek, rich
with fully paid flats and
fat retirement accounts—

that's the only excessively fat thing we want
our old people to have—we don't
think they should eat

so much fat, milk, honey, or white rice,
because diabetes is so costly—
not to mention unsightly

when the limbs get …
… abbreviated. Don't get us wrong,
we want our old to have long

lives of economic productivity
and if gluttony were good for that,
we would even encourage it.

Christine Chia

Quarantine

St John's Island

*There, amid beautiful Tembusu trees, stood some
government holiday bungalows ... [one] was ringed
with chain link topped with barbed wire. This housed
the political detainees.* —Lee Kuan Yew, 1952

Half an hour's sail from the shore, no more,
a square meal put away, a span of sleep
without dreaming. An island is a door

through which a sea is strung, famished lip
of land caught between the country's teeth,
a spool for the waves. This is how they keep

what must be kept at bay: on a reef
made fast with a brace of trees, like a fence
fine enough that it stays unseen, or a sieve,

not made to hold but to wear us thin. Once
our fathers came, fleeing death to death,
marooned so the barrenness would cleanse

their bodies' dread, while not a hand's breadth
away their betters ate and slept—exempt
by wealth or whiteness, more often both.

Now in their place, we who have neither bide
our time, nurse our hereditary rage,
watch for a turning in the southern tide

that daily scours this rock around the edge
and spares what springs unruly from the sand,
our banyan, mangrove, mastwood, sedge.

Theophilus Kwek

On Witnessing the Lindy Hop

At eight you were taken
by a demonstration of the Lindy Hop—
the way dancers tripped downwards,

backs to the floor, then bucked
themselves upright to the insistence
of fast trumpets, looking—for

brief moments— like they'd shook off
earthly patinas, ascended stairs
of breeze, could slingshot above

that curved lip of stage or space
until their swings became
an unplanned brushstroke smeared

across the gauzy weight of air,
were left suspended like a signature
ensconced in its corner

of some wilder universe where
you had yet to be betrayed
by gravity, and consequence, and jazz—

had time still to believe in the body
as a forward arc, rounding its stations,
never straining to escape itself.

Anurak Saelaow

We Are Slowly Dismantling Merit Bureaucracies

because as a matter of principle we're against bureaucracies, & merit
bureaucracies, & the very idea of merit. No one knows what merit is but we've
built whole structures of life on it & now our job 40 hours/week is to take it
apart. I'm in charge of file cabinets GHI and STU. You're in charge of ABC.
It's the largest file because some idiot wrote a long poem that was also an appeal
against exile that was also teenage wet dream that was also cry to God. Skimming
it made me sad. He was trying to imagine the world beyond and ended up in
the halls of a government office. Well none of that exists any longer. We are the
last bureaucrats existing only to kill bureaucracy forever. It's a tough job, you
have to have the stomach for it, to dig through denial and hierarchy and plea and
premature death and language that is a wall & is a stick. In these boxes the sticks
of language and the ghost *Wes*

> *We regret to inform you*
> *We are writing concerning claim no.* █████
> *We* █████ *up but you'll never know it*

Now you're reading the poem, the idiot's poem, despite my warnings. You're a
fast reader; you're already at the endnotes. You throw it into the shredder & we
both watch the humming teeth.

—And he barely ever even spoke to her in real life?
—Yeah, just kind of… looked from afar.
—What was he waiting for?
—Perhaps for a stamp of approval.
  Perhaps for the burgeoning of true desire.
  Perhaps for a sign that her desire was built like his desire, a massive burrow
of rooms filled with scurrying antpeople controlled by a massive unseen
intelligence.
—Desire like that doesn't exist.
—Ah but in days of old it was the only form they had of desire.

Ruth Tang

Dante in Singapore

Dante tours the Ten Courts of Hell

Haw Par Villa, Singapore

Past the gloomy stone arch sentried by
the ox guard with the trident and the horse
bearing the mace, I am surprised to spy
ten courts of hell instead of nine. Of course,
two deal with red tape, but the tortured cries
are ceaseless: rapists cook in boiling oil,
pickpockets are encased in blocks of ice,
and drug addicts like steaks are left to broil.
And when I see the sowers of discord
having their tongues ripped out, I think of how
back home they're mutilated. Here the sword
beheads the murderers, but I avow
we have tremendous commonality.
And yet, I'll bring some ideas home with me.

Dante endures the purgatory of Covid travel restrictions

Changi Airport, Singapore

Evening in Italy is here midnight.
Now I am locked down in this island state,
unable to depart. There is no flight
from here that lands at Fiumicino's gate,
beyond which you are. Somewhere in the hills
of Florence, the late rays of a setting orb
caress your cheek. The hint of summer fills
your heart the more, the more you can absorb.
But I am so far from your healing grace;
I can but look to when we beat this virus
and we can wrap ourselves in warm embrace.
That uncertain future can inspire us

though there is no shelter from that blight
that has robbed us of pure air and of sight.

Dante spots a beauty while playing the flâneur

Orchard Road, Singapore

As much as I can tell about that point,
just looking at her set my poor heart free
from other desires, for the light that joined
with her was an eternal ecstasy.
Her face so beautiful and rare
aroused the second aspect of my soul,
so much so I'd to stop my ambling there,
as though without her I could not be whole.
Vanquishing me with the light of a smile,
she said: 'Turn round and do not fantasise
but pay heed as you have done all this while,
for Paradise is not within my eyes.'
Easy for her to say. Hand her a mirror,
and watch her cool resolve begin to shiver.

Hsien Min Toh

Dante's Neapolitan

In the deep and bright
essence of that exalted Light, three circles
appeared to me; they had three different colors,
but all of them were of the same dimension
—Paradiso XXXIII.114–117

i strawberry

Not so the fear of finding a monster or the weft
of his mother's lost wool coat, a lover's imagined
laughter, smoke idling from abandoned altars,
but the manufactured taste of strawberries from
some chemical combination of colouring
and additives, tempered in a laboratory to catch
the possible tastes of strawberry, this tease at
an eternity of never apprehending the real thing.

ii vanilla

At first glance a plenary of sanitised hills, with
not even a chair to sit on, no consolation to
rest this scoop in, slips off tongue, forgettable
from first taste. The middle child of concoction,
neither here nor there, it exists so that others
might shine. But one should not stay for long,
enough prayer may send him to chocolate gates
of heaven or down to strawberry fields forever.

iii chocolate

This moderate pace of walking leads to promised
lands, an eternity gazing upon the mystery of the
holy cacao, endless days swimming in fondue
thickening with each swallow, infinite skies mark
the tempo of moving towards milky endings with
subtle hints of clementine, the aftertaste of
adventuring far from that dark wood to dwell
with his beloved in light that lingers from the stars.

Marc Nair

dante digestif singapura

'I'd rather sacrifice ninety-nine Singaporean souls than have to read Dante.'

I.

Ask for my name. Ask if, springless, I am ineloquent, Dante.

Favoured by Heaven, their light casts out your cowardice. Onward, Dante.

Wahlao, see la! Ask you choose faster. Get the Baygon, Dante.

Gas the lost lambs, hell-condemned. They died before they knew, Dante.

Your resentment immortalised ordinary lovers. Learn desire's cruel contradictions,
     wistful Dante.

Breathe in shit, hunger for power, take no prisoners. Andante, Dante.

When repentant and recalcitrant boil, you must serve them al, Dante.

But the only boatman in my heart is Charon, dear Dante.

Anything could lie beneath the veil—Read between your lines, Dante.

Cleave heretic body and soul before you leave this tomb, Dante.

Lay tightropes between man and demon, and make them walk, Dante.

Ride the beast across the boiling blood because you can, Dante.

Dead men do tell tales. Hear it through the grapevine, Dante.

Be true to yourself and design your most decadent Hell, Dante.

Follow your star, but beware the beasts attacking from both sides, Dante.

Old money is new money is old mon ... break the cycle, Dante!

Plunge, straddling venom, sheltered by his shoulders—your gratitude falters, Dante.

Fraudulent neanderthals / dumped into ditches / sinners deserve retribution / keep
     walking, Dante.

Look, upon this gold of God's perversion, how it scars, Dante!

Along your cantorial-contour, bestow divinity to destiny, men to Sisyphus, Dante!

Tremble not; even hell's steeper muscles retract for poetic licence, Dante!

Caught a bad fish, stand aside while I fork him, Dante!

Or space your strides till the difference overtakes my imagination, Dante.

Spite stings! Beware these mamba-fettered frauds on this serpent-festered plain,
     Dante!

Sinners silenced shedding skin, Faust deals evolution in pairs; denying Dante.

Ulysses, dream Joyce waxing Deleuze writing Kafka watching Virgil leading
     Dante!

Go and continue work with your faith that unearned dejecting, Dante!

'False' prophets, sowers of discord. Save that spot for Trump, Dante.
Disavow your gaze—aver your blood and pick your battles, Dante.
Dream of me as if I'm true, without an image, Dante.
Kina ah folgske tsao-khao Ho'mqi iahaI; shilok lah peruumal meria, Dante.
Leave your words—take only the cold beneath our tongues, Dante.
Unhinge the wolf's jaw and feed one traitor to another, Dante.

II.

All that remains is the unravelling of names: daybreak, desire, Dante.
May brothers reclaim, like shore and water, their last embrace, Dante!
To accept is to repent is to surely be saved, Dante.
Yet, egress transforms difficulty; how that returns to the same, Dante.
This kind of pain might unhouse a man his flesh, Dante.
Speaking about downfall precedes rebuilding, only if help comes for Dante.
Those who put Crown first, and Colony last: these too, Dante.
Losing love to a snake out of neglect oppressed souls, Dante.
Looking back at a sacred wall makes two both immigrants, Dante.
The humble honoured in relief, the proud toil without relief, Dante.
A portrait ciphered in yellow grass is still a portrait, Dante.
Left & right all the hao lian kenna rabak sia, Dante.
The lady (eyes wide shut) doth protest too much, methinks, Dante.
The Arno, like society, falls without fail, degenerates without stopping, Dante.
During that vapid morning, sick with sky, the cliff-face sighs, Dante.
Choice portrays both protagonist and antagonist; the stars, mere bit-players, Dante.
Fruit to pilgrim is crucifix, is prayer, is vapour blind, Dante.
A moon made mad with midnight is still a choice, Dante.
There's a power—when weakness and temptation awaken men's souls, Dante.
The taste of gold, the taste of gold is grief, Dante.
A simp meets his senpai and ooga booga sucky toe, Dante.
A coin teeters, spent; now a man meets his redeemer, Dante.
Time climbs upwards while a friend—beloved, beleaguered—cries, 'Dante.'
Men without death is food without hunger, love without desire, Dante.
Souls, without flesh, would still tempt comment on weight loss, Dante.
A woman cursed shouldn't burn for her inability to consent, Dante.
The fire-stung's prize was always this—the earth's spontaneous mirror—Dante.

Here's a screen-free space tended by an idealised woman, Dante.

The golden trees, the candle flames, lost in open shores, Dante.

Guides, loves and heart's desires: fatherly, motherly and beloved, elude Dante.

From bosom and water: emergence. Upon emergence: old gone, new Dante.

The apocalypse is still the apocalypse, no matter how beautiful, Dante.

Forgetting one has forgotten: trees rivers mountains grey with prophecy, Dante.

III.

Tell me, shall I lead her to your anointed body, Dante?

Across the sea, did the stars, their weight, consume you, Dante?

Penghuni bulan (walau sabit, walau mengambang) penghuni syurga juga, ya Dante?

Without doubt or differentiation, what grates the sea of being Dante?

The lawyers are calling. You've paid your dues, haven't you, Dante?

Is this the kind of standard you wanna give me, Dante?

But the just coexists in the unjust, haven't you noticed, Dante?

How come even in fanfic your sex so boring ah, Dante?

Why ask everyone's approval when it doesn't please your soul, Dante?

The corona of twelve souls interjected with viewpoints surrounding Trinity, Dante?

How did these burnished paths meet, or crown to equilibrium, Dante?

By this you recall the saints—how shall we remember Dante?

Find the centre, you said. But how many more circles, Dante?

The luminous red of Mars, like blood. Beautiful, isn't it, Dante?

Go35 go53 hai2 dai2 go5 li5 go3 hai2 sai3 go5. dan5te35?

An elegy that ages like a stillborn child—for you, Dante?

E queste parole, fioriranno dove i nostri corpi stanno decadendo, Dante?

Diligite iustitiam [squawk?] qui iudicatis terrammm [plane brrrrrrr]: spell, erase, dante.

M I B 4 H? U C D N? I Dante?

They fan embers not for sustenance but for wile faith, Dante!?

Now do you hear the music of paradise in silence, Dante?

Here you thought you'd climb a new sun didn't you, Dante?

This is Paradise? Can a poem leap to reach mirages, Dante?

Disrobe shadows, absent, abandoned—who spins your truth between judgement, Dante?

Shall we believe that one day we will return home, Dante?

By reason of desire does goodness thus / thus arise for Dante?
Where will you hide when the flower eats its fruit, Dante?
But what secures this spinning halo? What holds us now, Dante?
And if the angels turned, would you look their way, Dante?
Time begets the sea / radiant, longing godhood /spring sleeps, calls—Dante?
Which mortal movement shall preserve the rheumatoid contemplations of thunder,
    Dante?
Lilies stain the pinking shears. Can we bear His jagged ante?
And after this recursive pilgrimage, have you been made worthy, Dante?

Joshua Ip

INDIA

Inferno

Ciacco

To see a familiar, as though one were a wizard
    making their way through violent, energetic dimensions.
To see *them* suffer, in the dark marshes, is he still your enemy
    or friend, against the equalizing torque of death, afterdeath.
In my suffering, he suffers as *I,* does he still
    in that black world, need
his lesson?
  Ciacco is he, who predicts the victory of tyrants
within three hot suns; did he not once
    dream of love? Do the wicked not
dream of love?

Francesca

    Francesca, dearest, the things they accuse you of!
Jealousy, lust, incest, vanity, fie to all!
    Your sin was none but to forsake the myths
of your fathers, it was wanting life
    to be all your own, you were the hero
seeking absolution, in your own private hell. Desire
    does that for us: sets us free. And love?
Makes in us,
    something of the pure.

  O, Francesa, would you have taken
this poor pilgrim, and seen your face in his?
    If I found you before Paolo. If I held you in my eyes. You
Have done this before. Do it now. Soft as a dove.
  Be vain, I implore you. Beatrice
can wait.

Cerberus

Three-mouthed fiend, forever
    famished. What do I do but praise
the pain you endure, and what
    do I do, but see into your sixth eye, find your being
... and there it is: a cracked reflection
    of the holy trinity.

Medha Singh

Kashi after Dante

1. Bhuḥ

Don't ask who's cooking tonight

at Harischandra and Manikarnika
holy confidential kitchens of Kashi

Shroud tears, skin sears
Juicy fat's oblation

Did marrow fizz
Fire, laugh

In three hours and a half
this human log

collectable
in a dustpan

For the first time I think to
count your eyelashes

to pluck them
before they're singed

Of each I'll make a
boat unmoored

Where in the worlds
are you

As if I poured a sky
of wax on you

Everywhere you are not
your exact absence

2. Bhuvaḥ

In Uttarkashi

where sun dives and
pirouettes

and fish roll their eyes
dodging

tangled light doodles
We cup our hands

and drink Ma Ganga
infused

with arias of swans and
undertones of glaciers

Sweetness rises
Air floats sinless

In Kashi where

shadows hover anxious
like dogs marking

corners of terraced ghats
as lovers drink mirrors

A curly soot rains
upon the free bereft

and pundits claim
ashes still warm

from midnight pyres
for altar coffers at dawn

Hey Vishwanath of Kashi
O' Mt Alchemy

Here I am, weightless
Now take me home

3. Suvaḥ

So long as mountains meditate
this river will be wet

So long as boatmen paddle
a lullaby for the dead

Before sun strikes
and water turns cold

We row to a spot
churning upstream

Hand your ashes over
to the current

Ash can't swim

Hangs on to algae on hulls
Falls into arms of corals

Scraped and bitten by fish
Shat along gorges and flats

Why else do river beaches shine
What is mica made of

Mani Rao

Finding the Way

We ate the words. We were hungry.
We ate the words.

In the cave of our ancestors
we drank the wine of ritual,
sprinkled blood on the ground.
Who knows if it rained or snowed—
entangled in a myth
finding the way was hard
when we swallowed the sunrise and the sunset.

All the words were eaten.
What were the words, what was written?

In a dream the great hunter made a speech.
Come, he said, let us leave this torment of darkness
water and mist,
and sing for the river flowing east.
Undying on the wild way we followed
carrying the wind and waters,
the flying sky,
and the stag on the horizon
dancing among the stars.

Tomorrow—
would we reach tomorrow?

From the cave of our ancestors
the void continues to fill.
The letters of earth and sky
written in the outline of the hills:
a sun seed in the backbone,
the tenacity of grass;

root strength
and the fragrance of fleeting things,
the purpose of growing corn
and living mud
feeding breath with fire and bones
in the silence of our hills, the fury of our skies.

Mamang Dai

Lights, Camera, Dante!

Paradise Movie Theatre

INT. PARADISE MOVIE THEATRE: EVENING

The lobby at interval, its soft white clouds
lined with caramel; a rain of popcorn.
Coins fleeing my pocket like mice when I pay.

Yet a full scoop gifted by the kind winged vendor.
Like the film so far, friend, he asks.
I was living it, I tell him,

out of this world, that colour palette
a cosy cocoon of surround sound
those actors and actresses—their bods

and special effects as I've not seen before.
Here are my healed wounds that left
hardly a scar. What will the second half

do to me? A tap on my shoulder. I swivel.
The long face, the sharp nose, twinkling eyes.
No wings on him; a scroll unrolls at his feet.

Sequels are being shot, says the scriptwriter, Dante.
Who knows, you might land a role in them.
After this film, follow the scroll all the way down.

I tell him, *Been wishing for a life like a film.*
Watching this one has convinced me
that what I long for lies beyond my life.

Cleansing with the Stars

Curl, chamomile miasma, along the floor. *Done.*
Glow, neon runes, in the smog of our past. *Done.*
Put your scythe down, director, and set us

extras on our marks that look like crosses. *Done.*
Say Action. In the same breath, say Cut. *Done.*
Let the shooting begin and end timelessly. *Done.*

Capture us on film, twist it between your fingers. *Done.*
Let the stertorous intake of our breath be dank. *Done.*
Make us re-enact montages of our old times,

jump-cut sequences to be measured and gauged
which pop like wet wounds, stretching our skins.
Let each of our pores sprout a confessing tongue. *Done.*

Let our past coat the insides of our lungs … *Done.*
Let it flow in our breaths, drown our mouths … *Done.*
Purge repressed secrets from our bloodstream … *Done.*

Scrub them clean from our marrow. *Done.*
Have us face unwelcome strangers; ourselves—
so try as we may we can't avert our eyes. *Done.* Make us see

that greater than the pain of facing your sins
is the agony of being a self, that your name
is the tolling of an empty bell, nothing else. *Done.*

You say hamming, I say emoting. Potatoes, potahtos.
Promise me you won't take the scissors to my scene.
No guarantees. Post wrap up, please proceed to payments.

135

An Extra in the Inferno

I came to you
you gave me no lines
reservoirs of darkness
spill from my eyes
flow into my lungs
wash away traces

of bush fires
that crackled there
wash away charred
warped blackened
forms frozen
in terminal spasms

strewn across
a layer of ashes
amid standing husks
of tree trunks
darkness has fallen
at last I can sleep

when I hear
Cut!
and I return
to Paradise theatre
for a pittance
says the usher

the director's cut:
more roles available
no thanks I say
I must be going
I step out of the theatre
the theatre doesn't end

and I am back
in *Paradise*
there's been a mistake
the scriptwriter says
sorry
do the scenes again

I say
a meatier role please

Suhit Kelkar

Erasure

A hungry raven caws for bits of flesh—
the floods have laid out a feast. Someone
unfurls an unearthly wail. Death
has combed the sun from your hair.
A beast howls from behind my lungs.
There is so much I haven't told you.
When did we run out of time? Are you
just outside the periphery of my sight?
Are you merely sleeping
beyond the confines of language?
Are we together
but for the linearity of time?

*

The dog has stopped eating. The baby
whimpers hungrily in my milk-less chest.

Nirjala, remember you had once collected
my tear drops in your palms? You had promised
'I will come back from the dead for you'.

I light this lamp, the patheya, for you.
They say this flame guides the dead

on their journey onward. This one
will help show you your way back.

*

The government official stands—as usual—
safely away from the 'site of accident'
now hidden under fuming wet sand
for a moment before rushing off

to an important meeting with the Minister.
A dog yelps out of harm's way.

'Women do not work in coal mines'
so you did not make it to this list
of familiar names—the chosen ones
from all those who had walked into
the underground wearing their cracked
helmets and leaking gumboots.

Smita Sahay

Manikkavachakar's Space Odyssey

Argo's rocket fuel is exhausted. Solar panels dead. Communication lost.

I drift.

Below,
Earth spins in sapphire and nacre clouds, all allure.
Home's the place of no return.

Is this how I'll end my days? In a spaceboat directionless
amid thronged stars and scattered emptiness?

In velvet depths stars new-born shiver.
Rays from exploding suns quiver through the ship.

Flashes. Dashes. Orbital lidar streaks.
What's that oncoming blaze?

The woman who I created through song on another earth
approaches in her light.

Her shuttle docks with mine.

More beautiful than my ruby words
are her eyes as she drifts to me.

I'll guide you through the void. She slips
into Command. *Strap down. We enter warp speed.*

The familiar jolt through bone and marrow—and fresh this pierced heart.

Trust me, Siva-Anbu says. *Remember you
wrote about me. Intimately.*

A tribute, true to you.

My sex, you said, was a bud, its dark sepals
concealing petals of gold. You exposed me
to every reader. For which take this.

I'm shot into zero gravity.

Panels zoom close as mountains during descent.
Each knob a peak. Each screen a plateau.
I bruise myself on the quotidian.
Again. Again. Again. Again.

Okay. Descend.

I'm dumped into my seat. Ship's plunging through dazzle.
In this ceaseless shaft dimensions shift. Time laughs

When does this end?
It doesn't. She hums under her breath.

Calm descends.
Glow soft and brilliant, caresses like a kiss.
As through deep water, through some heavy thing, reflections ripple
each chiming like a note,
each pulsing joy.

She takes my hands. Binds them with threads of light. Blinds my eyes with rapture.
You body is the boat, Mann, get it?
Your only vehicle, your last solace.
You're the boatman too. And
the other shore. There's nothing more.
Man who utters ruby words—hear it sing.

In all my life, in all my journeys, this is all I've sought.
I weep cradled in endless love.

Priya Sarukkai Chabria

Fake News

As I often glimpsed paradise when alive
In the arms of women who let me come to them,
In a stream of clear water flowing down a hillside,
In butterflies over flowers, clouds in a blue sky,
In fireflies in the thickets of the night,
In the tears of those moved by pity, in their smiles,
In music, in song, in some paintings,
Yes, even, sometimes, in a slow conversation
With friends over beer and bread, I

Am certain, Devious Dante:
This is not paradise.

Tabish Khair

Juggler

You need help
            standing at attention
knapsack on back
on wave-thumped turf
you've got this far
            At first light
undeciphered time
            you're ready to start

*

Take it as it comes
            juggler
Look in the spice-grinder's vat
Mind
      your tricorne head
Here comes the iron
            thump
Watch it jump

*

Spar with prime numbers
Enter the castle
            through a loophole
Climb
      to the top of the horsemen's tower
Listen to the light
rain on the terrace
            If tigers could cry

*

Time
    to call back your powers
Pounce
      on saint-blessed cambric
      rivers traded for silver
      dormant ammonite
Look up
    for what comes next

Ranjit Hoskote

Paradiso

Angels in lycra glide by on the riverbank
the phalanx on the bicycle path repeated in black water

upside down. Drifting ducks vex that mindless orange synchrony
of pumping knees with bald impassive heads of iridescent green.

Ne-ver-the-less!—the ducks quack—should blood
well up on mown grass from a heroic last stand hereabouts

it is given to you to breathe in only the given moment.
A balsam poplar shakes out resplendent hair

leans into a magnolia in fragrant bloom
each great waxen chalice not proof of heaven

but heaven itself. The mallard chief becomes his feather cloak.
Three of his cohort ride the current, one paddles upstream

getting nowhere, two graze on a trove of duckweed bottoms up.
Midway through the latter end of life I find myself

drowsing in clover under an ancient willow
by a placid stream at the edge of the known world

beset by dandelions on the brink of paradise.

Irwin Allan Sealy

Through the *Mahabharata*'s Last Journey

Paradiso

Like Yudhishtra and his dog for paradise
first dragged through a hell where enemies
had been given time to rejoice
in their misdeeds or Dante gone to where Beatrice frees
him only after the descending circles
had penetrated earth's core and the breeze
of a limbo that combed and made continual ripples
in the emanations of beating heart,
sequence is the key to heaven's scruples:
sequence is what I've purposely taken apart
to know the movement of these bodies
with the indifference of their own light in the dark.
That which occurs here tarries
elsewhere, and that which does not occur occurs
nowhere else. Threw myself in flurries
to search for 'eternal calm'. Bore the worst
indignities. Faith is that thing born from hope and
the fiercest, cruelest imagination. There in the pursed
light, evolving, nucleosynthetic, had an opened
start so complete every single star
was a name. Token
of gratitude, the rush, the far-
thest sheen of names, and the name of the holy river
too, in celestial run. Avatar
of the historical arts, of grammar
and of the observant husbanded sciences
with the perfection of a poem but not its fatal tremor.
Then the end of all thought was also the coming of alliances
and the arrogant day-maker was no longer the sun,
the night's shepherd no longer the moon in all its glances.
Touch was the limit of theory, and theory and touch were one.

Vivek Narayanan

145

Notes

Hiroshima Triptych, pg 87

Quotations taken from Paul Tibbets, pilot of the plane that dropped the atomic bomb on Hiroshima, transcript C-Span, 1995.

Concatenation, pg 99

'Concatenation' includes a variation on Dante's line; 'All gates must spring aside.' Dante called rhyme *concatenation*; 'beautiful linkage'.
'Love-crumbs' is a phrase from EE Cummings' 'i like my body when it is with your'.

dante digestif singapura, pg 120

This poem is the collective work of 100 Singapore poets. Prelude: Joshua Ip; Inferno—1: Shawn Hoo; 2: Werner Kho; 3: Andrea Yew; 4: Samantha Toh; 5: Tommaso Federico Demarie; 6: Dennis Yeo; 7: Christopher Quek; 8: Drima Chakraborty; 9: Eva Lim; 10: Ian Chung; 11: Jolene Lum; 12: Kenneth Lim; 13: Leon Choo; 14: Nicolette Tan; 15: Ouyang Yingzhao; 16: Rohan Naidu; 17: Sandesh Kaur; 18: Abu Ubaidah; 19: Irie Aman; 20: Debabrota Basu; 21: Don Shiau; 22: Rajita Jay; 23: Kin Yunn; 24: Cee Zedby; 25: Bryan Ong Junyu; 26: Sean Francis Han; 27: Indah W. Yosevina; 28: Mark Goh; 29: Wahid Al Mamun; 30: Samuel Lee; 31: Hamid Roslan; 32: Teo Xiao Ting; 33: Rodrigo Dela Peña, Jr.; Purgatorio—1: Jerrold Yam; 2: Joses Ho; 3: Valen Lim; 4: Lune Loh; 5: Paul Jerusalem; 6: Jollin Tan; 7: Leonard Ng; 8: Eric Valles; 9: Crispin Rodrigues; 10: Joshua Lim; 11: Anurak Saelaow; 12: Dustin Wong; 13: Iain Lim; 14: Riqi Hanzrudyn; 15: Tan E-Reng; 16: Philip Greenall; 17: Hidhir Razak; 18: Jennifer Anne Champion; 19: Naicy Candido; 20: Elizabeth Fen Chen; 21: Skylar Yap; 22: Felix Deng; 23: Elizabeth Fong; 24: Yolanda Yu; 25: Karisa Poedjirahardjo; 26: Y-Lynn Ong; 27: Mrigaa Sethi; 28: Sharlene Teo; 29: Haidee Roiles; 30: Cheyenne Alexandria Phillips; 31: Pamela Seong Koon; 32: Faith Christine Lai; 33: Zhang Ruihe; Paradiso—1: Lee Jing-Jing; 2: Jonathan Chan; 3: Nabilah Said; 4: Michelle Tan; 5: Jia Han Tong; 6: Myko Philip; 7: Weiqi Chuah; 8: Tan Kuan Hian; 9: Lora Jane Arugay; 10: Irina Tjahjana; 11: Francine Wang; 12: Kevin Wong; 13: Migs Bravo-Dutt; 14: Arin Alycia Fong; 15: Margaret Louise Devadason; 16: Patricia Karunungan; 17: Jocelyn Suarez; 18: Michelle Lee; 19: Ashley Ho; 20: Muslim Sahib; 21: Inez Tan; 22: Nurul Amilin Hussain; 23: Sarah Mak; 24: Shalani Devi; 25: Amy Walter; 26: Al Lim; 27: Min Lim; 28: Jasmine Goh; 29: Letitia Chen; 30: Qamar Firdaus Saini; 31: David Wong; 32: Jack Xi; 33: Ally Chua.

Kashi after Dante, pg 129

Every day, hundreds of ritual cremations occur at Kashi's Manikarnika and Harishchandra *ghats* (banks). The mortal remains, i.e. the ashes, are then scattered in the river. The city's presiding deity is Shiva, called 'Vishwanath.' Some say the ash from midnight cremations is offered at the temple in the morning Our cosmos has seven worlds, regrouped into three—*bhuḥ* (earth), *bhuvaḥ* (an in-between realm), and *suvaḥ* (paradise, always a beach) (can't say which, it's private).

Finding the Way, pg 132

This is a reference to the lack of a writing system for the majority of tribes of Arunachal Pradesh. A large chunk of the customs and beliefs comes to us via the oral tradition with stories to explain the disappearance of a script that was written on animal skin. There is the story of an old man who possessed the history of his tribe written on deerskin but this got burnt and he ate it. In another version a deer that lived in the mountains saw the sons of a legendary ancestor writing the history of the world on a piece of liver. The deer approached them with an offer that men could write on his skin and he would give them back the letters whenever they needed them. However, during a hunt the men accidentally killed the deer and ate it.

Erasure, pg 137

from 'The Coal Miner of Jharia'

Manikkavachakar's Space Odyssey, pg 139

Prolific 9th century Tamil Saiva mystic Manikkavachakar is revered as the 'utterer of ruby words'. In his lesser known, eroticised and densely layered poem, *Thirukkovaiyar / Sacred Love Songs,* Manikkavachakar conceives Siva's compassion embody as the divinely beautiful woman, Siva-Anbu / Siva's Grace, who guides the seeker towards boundless love. In its secular reading the unnamed heroine of unsurpassed beauty is the prize the hero must win. The poem largely follows the structural conventions of Tamil Sangam (2BCE-4CE) poetics.

Contributors

Adam Aitken was born in London and spent his childhood in Thailand and Malaysia. He was Visiting Distinguished Professor at the University of Hawai'i and co-edited the *Contemporary Asian Australian Poets* anthology (Puncher & Wattmann, 2013). His latest collection, *Archipelago,* was shortlisted for the Prime Minister's Literary Award.

Amina Alyal has published poetry in journals and anthologies, and two collections, *The Ordinariness of Parrots* (Stairwell Books, 2015) and *Season of Myths* (Wordspace at Indigo Dreams, 2016), and academic publications. She teaches Creative Writing and English at Leeds Trinity University. She was editor of *Dream Catcher Magazine* in 2020.

Antonella Anedda (Anedda-Angioy), poet and essayist, studied in Venice and Oxford, where she earned a PhD with a thesis on Erasmus and Charles Darwin. Author of numerous volumes of poetry and winner of many prestigious awards, she has an honorary doctorate from the Sorbonne (2018). Her latest works are *Historiae* (poetry, Einaudi, 2018) and *Geografie* (prose, Garzanti, 2021).

Rossano Astremo is from Puglia, but has lived in Rome since 2007. He has published ten books, among them the poetry collections *Corpo poetico irrisolto* (Besa Editrice, 2003), *L'incanto delle macerie* (Icaro, 2007), and *Hai fatto burrasca* (Collettiva, 2020).

Cassandra Atherton is an award-winning prose poet and scholar of prose poetry. She was a Harvard Visiting Scholar in English and a Visiting Fellow at Sophia University. She co-authored *Prose Poetry: An Introduction* (Princeton University Press, 2020) and co-edited the *Anthology of Australian Prose Poetry* (Melbourne University Press, 2020). She is Professor of Writing and Literature at Deakin University.

Merlinda Bobis has twelve published books and ten dramatic works for stage and radio. She received the Christina Stead Prize for Fiction, three Philippine National Book Awards, and Steele Rudd Award (Best Collection of Australian Short Stories). She recently launched *The Kindness of Birds*, her new book of short stories.

Geoffrey Brock is the author of three books of poetry (most recently *Confluenze*), the translator of various books from various genres (most recently, *Allegria* by Giuseppe Ungaretti), and the editor of *The FSG Book of Twentieth-Century Italian Poetry*. He teaches creative writing and literary translation at the University of Arkansas.

Brian Brodeur is the author most recently of *Every Hour Is Late* (Measure Press, 2019). He teaches at Indiana University East.

Author of numerous poetry collections and winner of many prestigious awards, **Franco Buffoni** (b. Gallarete, 1948) is full professor of literary criticism and comparative literature. For 30 years he taught at the universities of Bergamo, Cassino, Milano IULM, Parma and Torino. He founded (and is still editor) of the review *Testo a fronte.*

Adrian Caesar has published six books of poetry, including *This Cathedral Grief* (Recent Work Press, 2020). He has written several books of literary criticism and an award-winning non-fiction novel, *The White.* His novel, *The Blessing,* was long-listed for the Voss Award in 2016. Another novel, *A Winter Sowing,* is due for publication in September 2021.

Scott Cairns is Professor of English and Director of Creative Writing at Seattle Pacific University. His most recent books are *Slow Pilgrim: The Collected Poems* (2015) and *Anaphora: New Poems* (2019).

Matthew Caley's sixth full-length collection is *Trawlerman's Turquoise* (Bloodaxe, 2019). He gave the StAnza Lecture 2020 when *Trawl,* a video made with Steve Smart and Alex South, was shown throughout the festival, and since, at poem–film festivals in Berlin and Texas. *Prophecy is Easy*, a pamphlet of loose versions from French poets, came out from Blueprint Press in February 2021.

Siobhán Campbell is the author of six books of poetry and co-editor of *Eavan Boland: Inside History,* the 2016 book of essays on the work of Eavan Boland. Her work has received awards in the National Poetry Competition and the Troubadour International Competition, also an Arts Council award and the Templar Poetry Prize.

Vahni Capildeo is a Trinidadian Scottish writer who has published seven books (and four pamphlets) including *Measures of Expatriation,* awarded the Forward Prize for Best Collection in 2016 and shortlisted for the TS Eliot Prize that same year.

Priya Sarukkai Chabria is an award-winning poet, translator, and writer of speculative fiction and literary non-fiction. Her books include *Sing of Life: Revisioning Tagore's Gitanjali* (Context, 2021) and other poetry collections; speculative fiction *Clone* (Zubaan, University of Chicago Press) and translations of the 9th century Tamil poet-mystic, *Andal: The Autobiography of a Goddess* (Zubaan, University of Chicago Press). She's Founding Editor, *Poetry at Sangam.* *poetry.sanghamhouse.org*

Bryan Cheong is from Singapore, and currently resides in San Francisco. His work has previously appeared in *QLRS*, the *Istanbul Review*, the *Asia Literary Review*, and other magazines and anthologies. He was the inaugural recipient of Stanford University's Wiley Birkhofer prize for poetry.

Christine Chia is the author of *The Law of Second Marriages* (Math Paper Press) and a sequel, *Separation: a history* (Ethos Books). She co-edited the groundbreaking anthology *A Luxury We Cannot Afford* (Math Paper Press, 2014) and a sequel, *A Luxury We Must Afford* (2016). Her first full-length play was read at Centre 42's First Acts programme and she is working on her third poetry collection.

Jane Clarke has pubished two collections, *The River* (Bloodaxe, 2015), which was shortlisted for the 2016 Royal Society of Literature's Ondaatje Prize, and *When the Tree Falls* (Bloodaxe, 2019). Her illustrated chapbook *All the Way Home* (Smith|Doorstop, 2019) responds to a World War I archive of letters and photographs held in the Mary Evans Picture Library, London.

Katharine Coles' new book of essays is *The Stranger I Become: On Walking, Looking, and Writing*. She has received awards from the (US) National Endowment for the Arts, National Endowment for the Humanities, National Science Foundation, and Guggenheim Foundation. She is a Distinguished Professor at the University of Utah.

Judith Nangala Crispin is a poet and visual artist, of Bpangerang descent, and former poetry editor of the *Canberra Times*. She lives near Lake George and has two published collections of poems, *The Myrrh-Bearers* (Puncher & Wattmann, 2015) and *The Lumen Seed* (Daylight Books, 2017).

Mamang Dai is a poet and novelist from Arunachal Pradesh. A former journalist, Dai also worked with WWF in the Eastern Himalaya Biodiversity Hotspots programme. In 2011 Dai was awarded the Padma Shri, and in 2017 the Sahitya Akademi Award for her book *The Black Hill*.

Maura Dooley's most recent collection is *The Silvering* (Bloodaxe, 2016). She teaches at Goldsmiths, University of London and she is a Fellow of the Royal Society of Literature.

Moira Egan has published five collections of poetry in the US and three in Italy. A new bilingual volume is forthcoming (Tlön, Rome, 2022). Her work has appeared in journals and anthologies on four continents. With her husband, Damiano Abeni, she has translated many American poets into Italian. She lives in Rome.

Paolo Febbraro (b. Roma 1965) has published six poetry collections and *Il Diario di Kaspar Hauser,* a work in prose and poetry. His work has been translated into many languages and his short prose pieces are collected in *I grandi fatti.* His critical works focus on Seamus Heaney.

D. W. Fenza is the author of *The Interlude,* a book-length poem. For three decades, he worked as an editor and then as director for the Association of Writers & Writing Programs (AWP).

Cindy Frenkel's *The Plague of the Tender-Hearted* was published last year. '15 Lessons from 9 Years of Teaching' appeared in *Writing in Education* and 'Galway Kinnell and the Blue Button-Down' in *The Southampton Review.* Recently, she wrote for *WIRED* about teaching writing for video gamers. www.cindyfrenkel. com

Massimo Gezzi (b. 1976) has published a short-story collection, *Le stelle vicine* (Bollati Boringhieri, 2021), and poetry collections, *Il mare a destra* (Atelier, 2004), *L'attimo dopo* (luca sossella editore, 2009), *Il numero dei vivi* (Donzelli Editore, 2015) and *Uno di nessuno: Storia di Giovanni Antonelli, poeta* (Edizioni Casagrande, 2016). He lives in Lugano.

Marco Giovenale founded the website gammm.org in 2006. He is the author of numerous poetry collections and his work has appeared in many anthologies, including the collective book, *Prosa in prosa* (Le Lettere, 2009). He translated *Billy the Kid* by Jack Spicer (Camera Verde, 2018).

Franca Grisoni (b. Sirmione 1945) has won the Bagutta and Viareggio Poetry Prizes. Her collections include *Crus d'amur* (Interlinea, 2016) and *Il filo srotolato* (Morcelliana, 2021). She has also published works for theatre (*Passiù,* 2008; *Medea,* 2012), essays, and the anthology *Alzheimer d'amore* (2017).

Philip Gross has published some twenty collections of poetry, most recently *Between The Islands* (Bloodaxe, 2020). He is a keen collaborator—with poet Lesley Saunders on *A Part of the Main* (Mulfran, 2018) and with Welsh-language poet Cyril Jones and artist Valerie Coffin Price on the bilingual *Troeon/Turnings* (Seren, 2021). www.philipgross.co.uk

Oz Hardwick is a widely published European poet and medievalist, whose most recent publication is the prose poetry sequence *Wolf Planet* (Hedgehog, 2020). Oz is Professor of English at Leeds Trinity University, where he leads the postgraduate Creative Writing programmes. www.ozhardwick.co.uk

Nick Havely is Emeritus Professor at the University of York. His recent publications include *Dante's British Public* (OUP, 2014) and a new translation of the *Purgatorio* by contemporary poets (Arc Publications, 2021). He has received Leverhulme and Bogliasco Fellowships and is an Honorary Member of the Dante Society of America.

Paul Hetherington is a distinguished Australian poet who has won or been nominated for over thirty national and international awards. He is Professor of Writing at the University of Canberra, head of the International Poetry Studies Institute and founder of the International Prose Poetry Group. He is co-author of *Prose Poetry: An Introduction* (Princeton University Press, 2020).

Eleanor Hooker's debut, *The Shadow Owner's Companion* (Dedalus Press) was shortlisted for the Strong/Shine Award for Best First Irish Collection of 2012. Her third poetry collection and two poetry chapbooks are due for publication in 2021. She is a recipient of the prestigious Markievicz Award from the Arts Council of Ireland 2021.

Ranjit Hoskote's collections of poetry include *Vanishing Acts* (Penguin, 2006), *Central Time* (Penguin, 2014), *Jonahwhale* (Penguin, 2018; in the UK by Arc as *The Atlas of Lost Beliefs*, 2020), and *Hunchprose* (Penguin, 2021). His translation of a 14th-century Kashmiri woman mystic's poetry has appeared as *I, Lalla: The Poems of Lal Ded* (Penguin Classics, 2011).

Joshua Ip is a Singaporean poet, editor and literary organiser. He has published four poetry collections, edited ten anthologies, and co-founded Sing Lit Station, an over-active literary charity. His latest collection of anachronistic translations of Tang Poetry, *translations to the tanglish*, is forthcoming with Math Paper Press in 2021. joshuaip.com

Mark Jarman's latest books are *The Heronry*, a collection of poetry, and *Dailiness: Essays on Poetry*. He lives in Nashville, Tennessee.

Judy Johnson has published five full-length books of poetry. She has won major awards for both single poems and collections. Her latest work, *Dark Convicts* is a poetic narrative dealing with the life and times of her two First Fleet African American ancestors.

Suhit Kelkar is a writer and photographer based in Mumbai. His poems and journalism appear in India and abroad. He has two chapbooks: *The Centaur Chronicles* explores otherness, discrimination, weirdness; *Mumbai Monochrome* combines photos and haiku/senryu to reveal a quieter side of Mumbai. Suhit tweets @suhitkelkar.

Tabish Khair, born in 1966 and educated in Bihar, India, is the author of critically-acclaimed books, including the novels, *The Bus Stopped, Filming*, and *Night of Happiness*. Winner of the All India Poetry Prize, his novels have been shortlisted for more than a dozen prizes.

Theophilus Kwek has published four collections of poetry, two of which were shortlisted for the Singapore Literature Prize. The most recent is *Moving House* (Carcanet, 2020). He has also been awarded the New Poets' Prize, Jane Martin Prize, Berfrois Poetry Prize, and Stephen Spender Prize for poetry in translation. He currently serves as poetry editor of the *Asian Books Blog*.

Jerome Lim's writing has been published in the *Quarterly Literary Review Singapore, The Mays, Sloth*, and the *Journal of Modern Literature*, amongst others. He is the managing editor of *Error! Hyperlink reference not valid.*, and his poetic sequence *Archipelago* was awarded the Ursula Wadey Memorial Prize in 2018.

Miriam Wei Wei Lo teaches creative writing in Perth, Australia. After raising three children in a country town and doing the unpaid work of a pastor's wife, Miriam is thrilled to live in a city with a train that takes her to work at the Sheridan Institute. Find her on Insta @miriamweiweilo.

Glyn Maxwell has won several awards, including the Somerset Maugham Prize, the EM Forster Prize and the Geoffrey Faber Memorial Prize. His plays have been staged in the UK and USA, and he has written libretti for major operas. His most recent collection is *How the hell are you* (Picador, 2020).

Catherine Phil MacCarthy was Writer in Residence for the City of Dublin in 1994. She received the eighteenth Lawrence O'Shaughnessy Award for Poetry of the University of St Thomas Center for Irish Studies in April 2014. The Arts Council, An Comhairle Ealaíon, has awarded her a Bursary towards each of her poetry collections. She is a former editor of *Poetry Ireland Review*.

Thomas McCarthy has published many collections of poetry, also two novels and two works of non-fiction. His *Pandemonium* was published by Carcanet in 2016 and was short-listed for the *Irish Times*/Poetry Now Award. He has won the Patrick Kavanagh Award, the Alice Hunt Bartlett Prize and the O'Shaughnessy Prize for Poetry.

Maria McManus was born in Enniskillen and lives in Belfast. Her debut collection, *Reading the Dog* (Lagan Press), was shortlisted for the 2007 Strong/Shine Award and Glen Dimplex New Writers Award. Her latest collection, *Available Light*, was released by Arlen House in 2018. She is artistic director of the Poetry Jukebox.

Paul Munden is a poet, editor and screenwriter living in North Yorkshire. Formerly Director of the UK's National Association of Writers in Education, he is an Adjunct Associate Professor at the University of Canberra. www.paulmunden.com

Marc Nair is a poet who works at the intersection of art forms. He is currently pursuing projects that involve photography and creative non-fiction. His work revolves around the ironies and idiosyncrasies of everyday life. He has published ten collections of poetry.

Vivek Narayanan's most recent book of poems is the forthcoming *AFTER: A Writing Through Valmiki's Ramayana*, to be published internationally by the *New York Review of Books* and in India by HarperCollins.

Eiléan Ní Chuilleanáin has spent her working life as an academic in Trinity College, Dublin. She has won the Patrick Kavanagh Award, the *Irish Times* Award for Poetry, the O'Shaughnessy Award of the Irish-American Cultural Institute, and the International Griffin Poetry Prize. Her *Collected Poems* was published in October 2020.

Mary O'Donnell's eight poetry collections include *Those April Fevers* (Arc Publications, 2015) and *Massacre of the Birds* (Salmon Poetry, 2020). She has also published novels and short story collections. A volume of essays on her work, *Giving Shape to the Moment: The Art of Mary O'Donnell*, was published in 2018 (Peter Lang).

Nessa O'Mahony has published five volumes of poetry, the most recent being *The Hollow Woman on the Island* (Salmon Poetry 2019). She is co-editor, with Paul Munden, of *Metamorphic: 21st century poets respond to Ovid* (Recent Work Press, 2017). Recent co-editions include *Empty House* (Doire Press, 2021) and *Days of Clear Light* (Salmon Poetry, 2021).

Jacqueline Osherow is the author of eight collections of poetry, most recently *My Lookalike at the Krishna Temple* (LSU Press, 2019). She's received Guggenheim, NEA and Ingram Merrill Foundation Fellowships and the Witter Bynner Prize. She's Distinguished Professor of English at the University of Utah.

Alvin Pang is a Singaporean poet and editor whose writing has been translated into more than twenty languages worldwide. His recent books include *What Happened: Poems 1997-2017* (2017) and *Uninterrupted time* (2019). An Adjunct Professor of RMIT University, he translated two Cantos for the anthology *After Dante: Poets in Purgatory* (2021).

Felicity Plunkett is an award-winning poet and critic. She is the author of *A Kinder Sea* (UQP, 2020), *Vanishing Point* (UQP, 2009) and the chapbook *Seastrands* (2011), published in Vagabond Press' Rare Objects series. She edited *Thirty Australian Poets* (UQP, 2011).

Craig Raine is a poet, novelist, playwright, literary critic and editor. His most recent book is *My Grandmother's Glass Eye – a Look at Poetry* (2016).

Mani Rao's poetry books include *Sing to Me* (Recent Work Press), *New & Selected Poems* (Poetrywala) and *Echolocation* (Math Paper Press). Her translations from Sanskrit include *Bhagavad Gita* and *Kalidasa for the 21st Century Reader*. *Living Mantra: Mantra, Deity and Visionary Experience Today* (Palgrave Macmillan) is her latest non-fiction. manirao.com

Anurak Saelaow has been published in *Cha: An Asian Literary Journal, Hayden's Ferry Review, Quarterly Literary Review Singapore, Cultural Weekly, The Kindling, Ceriph*, and elsewhere. He is the author of one chapbook, *Schema* (The Operating System, 2015), and holds a BA in creative writing and English from Columbia University.

Smita Sahay's writings have appeared in national and international publications. She is a Founding Co-editor, *Usawa Literary Review,* Associate Editor, *Veils, Halos & Shackles: International Poetry on the Oppression and Empowerment of Women,* and Poetry Editor, *Speak.* She is working on poems on the underground coalfield fires in Jharia, Jharkhand.

Fiona Sampson MBE FRSL is a leading British poet and writer, critic, librettist and literary biographer, who is published in thirty-seven languages and the recipient of numerous national and international awards. She is Emeritus Professor of Poetry, University of Roehampton.

Will Schutt is the author of *Westerly* and translator of Andrea Marcolongo's *The Ingenious Language*, Renzo and Carlo Piano's *Atlantis*, and *My Life, I Lapped It Up: Selected Poems of Edoardo Sanguineti*. His many awards include the 2012 Yale Younger Poets Prize and the 2019 Raiziss/de Palchi Fellowship for translations of Fabio Pusterla's poems.

Irwin Allan Sealy is the author of *The Trotternama* and other novels, and the travel books *Yukon to Yucatan* and the *China Sketchbook Zelaldinus* is a cycle of Akbar poems. A memoir, *The Small Wild Goose Pagoda*, is set in his hometown, Dehra Dun. *Asoca: a sutra* was published this year.

Medha Singh is a poet, translator and editor. Her books are *Ecdysis* (Poetrywala, 2017) and a translation of Indian painter S.H. Raza's love letters from the French, *I Will Bring My Time: Love Letters by S.H. Raza* (Vadehra Art Gallery, 2020). She is editor of *Berfrois*.

Alex Skovron's publications include seven collections of poetry, a prose novella and a volume of short stories. *Towards the Equator* (2014), his new and selected poems, was shortlisted in the Australian Prime Minister's Literary Awards. His latest collection, *Letters from the Periphery* (2021), includes a translation of Canto 1 from *Inferno*.

Jean Sprackland's latest collection is *Green Noise* (Cape, 2018), and in 2020 she published *These Silent Mansions*, a book about graveyards. She was the winner of the Costa Poetry Award in 2008, and the Portico Prize for Non-Fiction in 2012. Jean lives in London, and is Professor of Creative Writing at Manchester Metropolitan University.

Janet Sylvester's third book, *And Not to Break*, won the Lauria/Frasca Poetry Prize in 2019 and was published by Bordighera Press (NYC) in 2020. An introductory section of 'Beatrice in Exile' was first published as a single poem, 'Courtesy', in *And Not to Break*.

Marylyn Tan is a linguistics graduate, poet, and artist interested in conditions of alienation and marginalisation. The founder of arts collective DIS/CONTENT (hellodiscontent.carrd.co), her writing has been featured in various print anthologies. *Gaze Back*, her first published book, won the 2020 Singapore Literature Prize for English Poetry.

Ruth Tang is a playwright, poet and maker of weird internet experiments, raised in Singapore and presently living in Brooklyn, NY. Their other preoccupations include bargain basement books, long aimless walks, and slowly learning how to fix bikes.

Hsien Min Toh has authored four books of poetry, most recently *Dans quel sens tombent les feuilles* (Paris, 2016), and is the founding editor of the *Quarterly Literary Review Singapore*. His work has also recently been published in *Arc Poetry Magazine*, *SAND Journal* and *The Stinging Fly*.

Sidney Wade's most recent book is *Deep Gossip: New & Selected Poems*, from the Johns Hopkins University Press. She lives in Rangeley, Maine and Gainesville, Florida.

William Wall was the 2017 winner of the Drue Heinz Prize for Literature (USA). Other prizes won include the Premio Lerici-Pea 'AngloLiguria' prize (Italy) and The Patrick Kavanagh Award (Ireland). He has a particular interest in Italy and has read at several festivals there. He was the first Poet Laureate of Cork (2021–22).

Kimberly K. Williams is the author of two books of poetry, *Sometimes a Woman* (Recent Work Press) and *Finally, the Moon* (SFA University Press). Kimberly's poems appear in journals and anthologies around the world. She is currently working on a PhD at the University of Canberra and is originally from Detroit, Michigan.

Joseph Woods was Poetry Ireland's longest serving director until 2013. His first collection, *Sailing to Hokkaido* (Worple Press, 2001) was awarded the Patrick Kavanagh Poetry Award. His fourth collection *Monsoon Diary* (Dedalus Press, 2018) is based in part on his experience of living in Burma. He now lives in Harare, Zimbabwe.

Lightning Source UK Ltd.
Milton Keynes UK
UKHW011418180921
390797UK00003B/82